SCALES & MODES IN THE BEGINNING

CREATED ESPECIALLY FOR GUITARISTS

BY RON MIDDLEBROOK

Editing George Ports
Calligraphy George Ports
Cover Art Don Hendricks
Cover Lettering Steve Kniepp
Layout, Design, and Production Ron Middlebrook

ISBN: 978-0-89898-151-3

Beefs

P.O. BOX 17878 ANAHEIM HILLS, CA 92807 USA

CONTENTS

CONTENTS

IMPROVISING

One of the biggest stumbling blocks on the road to the town of great guitar playing is the improvised solo. Be it rock, jazz, pop, country, or whatever. We might ask, why do so many good musicians use scales to their benefit and avoid sounding too diatonic, boring, lifeless, contrived or mechanical? You'll hear them playing super solos that are (at least in part) based on these same scales contained in this book. The Secret! They experiment, change, alter, and use their imagination and most important they use them in the right places, at the right time, in other words making the scale appropriate to the musical setting.

Our purpose of this book is to present in an easy and as concise form as possible for the guitarist, the scales that are used in improvisation.

Our objective is to find a level where our musical intuitiveness can express itself on our instrument.

Our goal then is this: practicing exercises, patterns, licks, scales, and chords should lead to more expressive creativity.

Anyone can improvise, it's just that many of us think we can't. Be positive! Start out playing short phrases. (Two bar phrases would be fine). Remember, a positive mental attitude is essential to successful improvisation.

ABOUT THIS BOOK

This book is divided into four basic sections:

1.FRETBOARD VISUALIZATIONS
(We have to know the fretboard)

2. SCALE TERMINOLOGY
(We have to know what we're talking about)

3. THE SCALES AND MODES
Every scale you'll want to know. Along with the scale are explanations as to the application of the scale form to one or more chord types. And showing the relationship of certain scales to each other. Plus several pages on arpeggios.

4. This last section brings it all together with a handy "scale to chord guide" that will be a valuable aid in memorization.

GENERAL NOTES

1. Play it correct the first time. This is most important. Before you touch a fret, play it mentally, then very slowly play the scale. Make that first run through correct.

2. The words scale and modes mean the same thing.

3. Accuracy not speed is important.

4. Play each scale forward and backward.

5. Pick 3 ways, all up, all down, and alternating down and up.

6. Start out slow and gradually build up speed. To challenge yourself set a time limit, of say playing the pattern forward and backward in under 10 seconds.

7. All the scales in this book are movable and should be played in all keys, up and down the fretboard.

8. The scales in this book are not arranged in order of difficulty or importance but just what seem to be logical categories.

Hand Positions
Right Hand or Picking Hand

1. Experiment with different types and thicknesses of picks. General rule, thicker pick--mellow sound, thinner pick--treble sound. Most players prefer a medium pick.

2. Avoid to much arching of the wrist.

3. Avoid any kind of anchor that restricts freedom of movement. A little bit of an anchor for certain sounds or picking is O.K. For the most part "keep it loose", be flexible.

Hand Positions
Left Hand or Fretting Hand

1. Fingers should be arched, knuckles bent.

2. The finger should move straight up and down on the strings, like little hammers, at a right angle to the fretboard.

3. Lift the fingers just high enough to clear the strings, too high is wasted motion.

4. The thumb should ride approximately at the center of the back of the neck. Try to maintain a consistent relationship with the second finger.

Both Hands Working Together

The left and right hand must work in perfect synchronization. If the pick attacks first and the finger follows, you'll hear two sounds, not good. If the finger attacks first and the pick follows, again two sounds, still not good. You must pick and finger the note at exactly the same time. To reach that goal, play very slowly when you start to practice the scales or anything you like to play. Concentrating only on picking and fingering that note at the same time. Remember we're not looking for speed here, it's technique.

1 SECTION

FRETBOARD VISUALIZATION

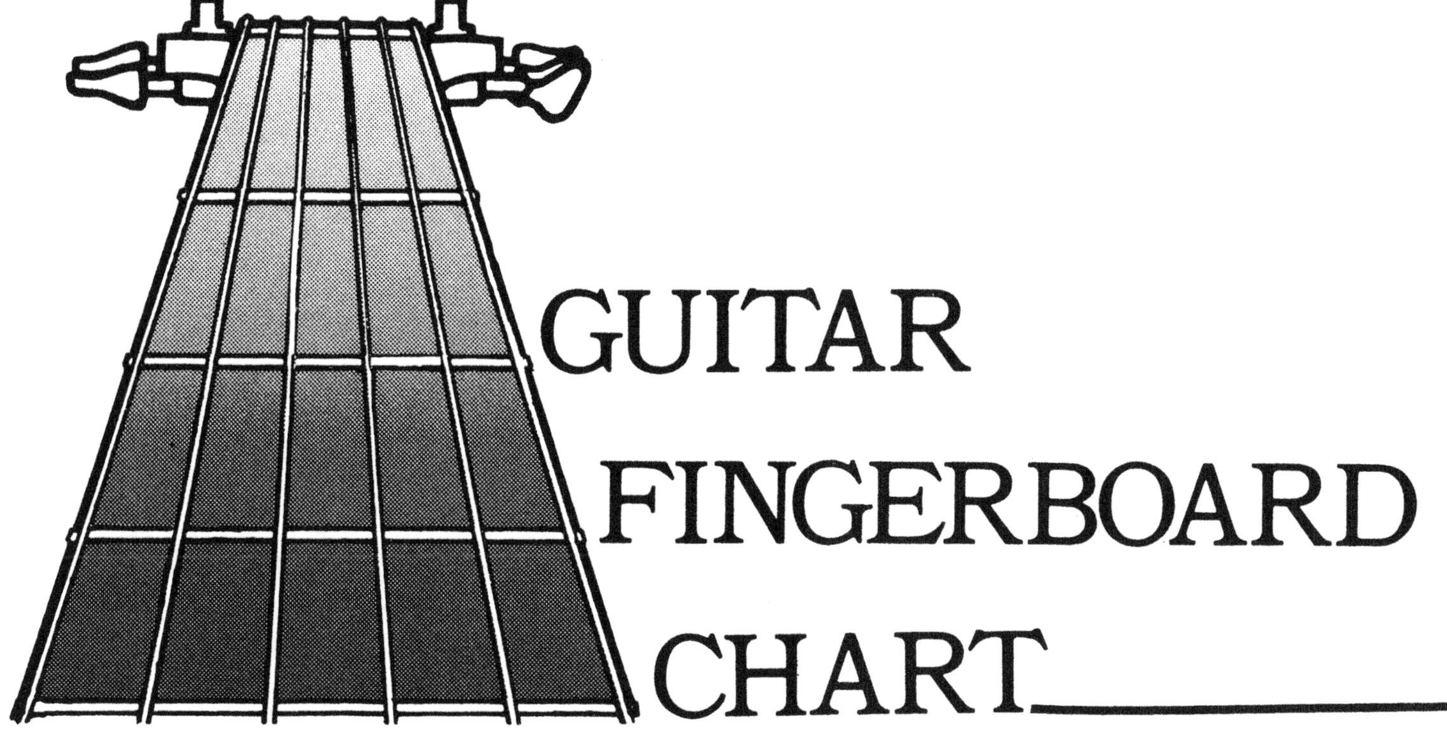

GUITAR FINGERBOARD CHART

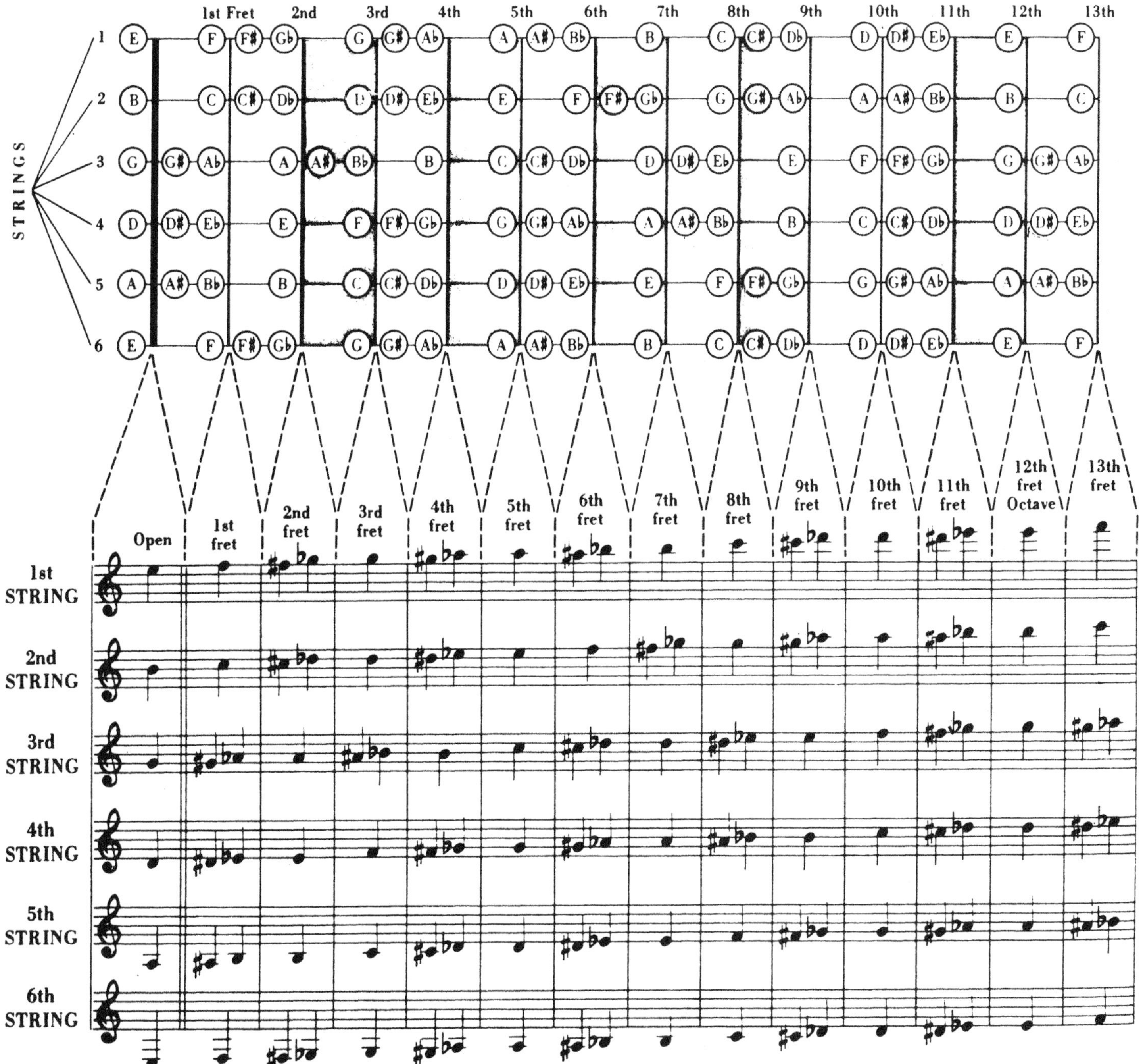

STRINGS

String	Open	1st Fret	2nd	3rd	4th	5th	6th	7th	8th	9th	10th	11th	12th	13th
1	E	F	F# Gb	G	G# Ab	A	A# Bb	B	C	C# Db	D	D# Eb	E	F
2	B	C	C# Db	D	D# Eb	E	F	F# Gb	G	G# Ab	A	A# Bb	B	C
3	G	G# Ab	A	A# Bb	B	C	C# Db	D	D# Eb	E	F	F# Gb	G	G# Ab
4	D	D# Eb	E	F	F# Gb	G	G# Ab	A	A# Bb	B	C	C# Db	D	D# Eb
5	A	A# Bb	B	C	C# Db	D	D# Eb	E	F	F# Gb	G	G# Ab	A	A# Bb
6	E	F	F# Gb	G	G# Ab	A	A# Bb	B	C	C# Db	D	D# Eb	E	F

Open | 1st fret | 2nd fret | 3rd fret | 4th fret | 5th fret | 6th fret | 7th fret | 8th fret | 9th fret | 10th fret | 11th fret | 12th fret Octave | 13th fret

1st STRING

2nd STRING

3rd STRING

4th STRING

5th STRING

6th STRING

Fretboard Visualization

The eventual goal is total fretboard awareness and freedom. It must ultimately be cultivated and achieved within the mind and away from your instrument. "Visualization is the key". Look at figure 1, it's all the notes available to us in the C major scale up to the 12th fret.

Figure 1

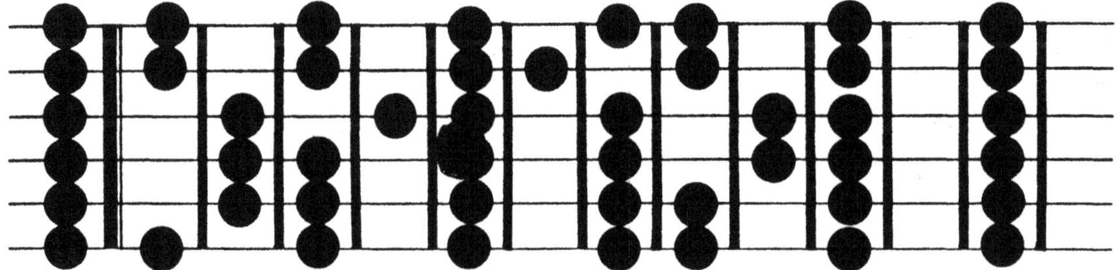

The challenge for all of us is illustrated in the above example by the overwhelming choice of notes (in the key of C). To compound it you might know that we can play the open first string "E" pitch in five different locations. Whereas a keyboard player in comparison finds this same pitch on one key and one key only.

This duplication of pitches on guitar is one of the greatest performing advantages, but at the same time one of the biggest learning disadvantages of the instrument. So out of survival some schools of fretboard perception have been created. The breaking down of the whole into parts. Let's explore some of them.

SEGOVIAN FINGERINGS

Andres Segovia has suggested a series of fingering patterns in his 12 page book "Diatonic Major and Minor Scales" published by Columbia Music Co. P.O. Box 19126, Washington, D.C. 20036.

The Segovian fingerings are linear (up and down the length of the fretboard) rather than lateral (across the fretboard). See chromatic exercises.

THE THREE NOTES PER STRING CONCEPT

Practiced by the Johnny Smith, George Van Eps, George M. Smith school of thought. Here the seven major scale shapes are designed using three notes per string with the starting note of each shape based on each one of the seven diatonic pitches. Do-Re-Mi-Fa-Sol-La-Ti-Do or as in scale step numerology; 1-2-3-4-5-6-7. The following examples illustrate the three-notes-per-string concept.

The entire fingerboard is covered in the seven positions. Each fingering has a different note as its lowest reachable note. (the root note is the square note)

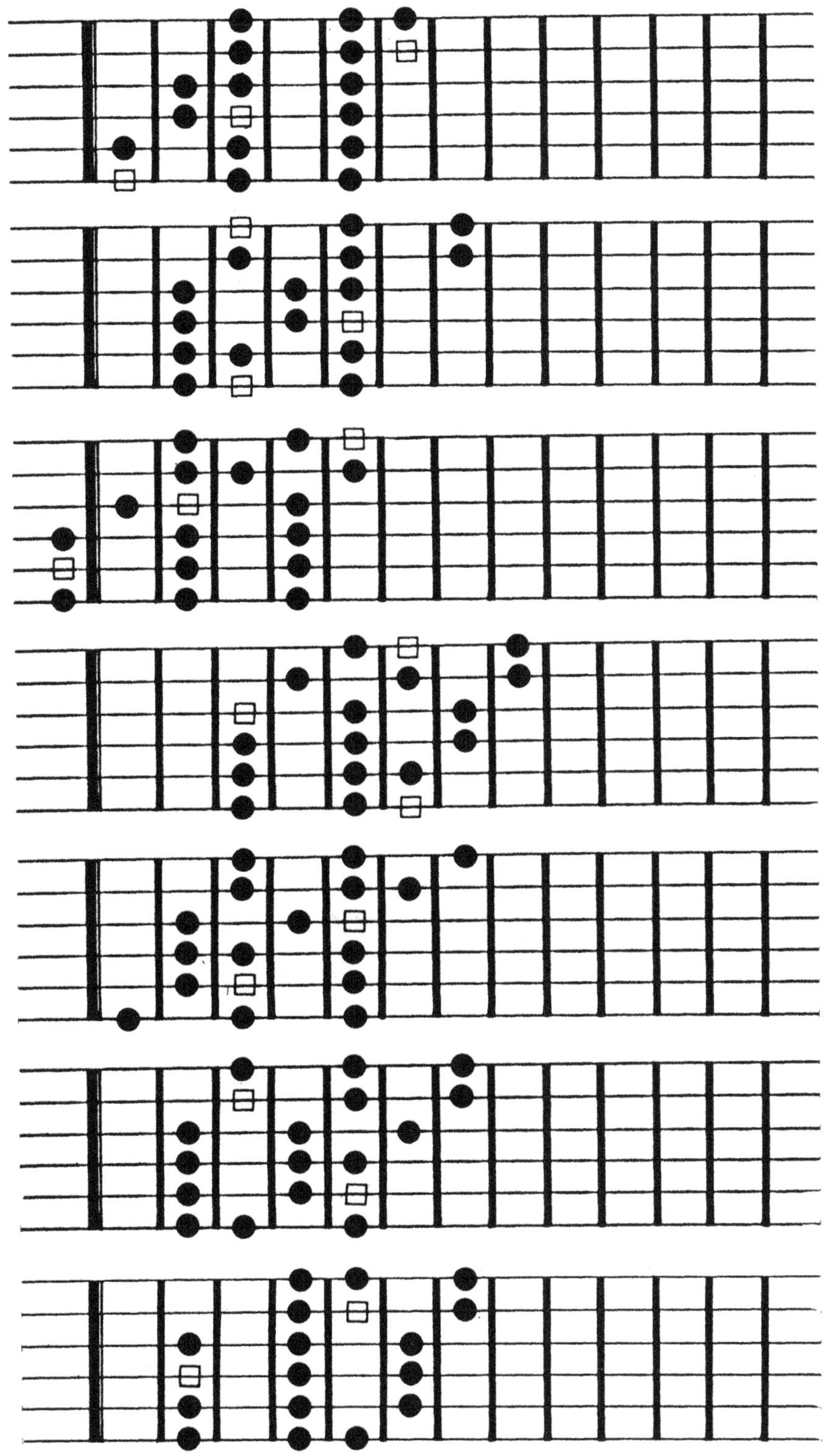

THE CAGED SYSTEM

Coined by the late L.A. studio player/composer Jack Marshall is based on the five chord shapes found in the open position,i e. C, A, G, E, D, used by such pros as Howard Roberts, Barney Kessel, and Herb Ellis.

The fingerings center around the use of a finger per fret. However in some of the patterns you may have to reach out of position one fret above or below the basic position.

All of the patterns can be moved up or down the fingerboard for access to any key and all other scales can be made by modifications of these diatonic patterns.

Laying these patterns end to end they cover the entire fretboard for any one key.

As with the 3 note-per-string fingering, all other scales can be produced through modifications of these diatonic patterns.

Each pattern starts with the lowest available note in the range of the pattern going to the highest (not from tonic to tonic) the tonics are circled.

Also, arpeggios will be easier to handle if they are played within a scale pattern corresponding to the key center from which the chord is derived, i.e.; the progression Em7, Am7, Dm7, and G7, is a III, VI, II,and V progression in the key of C.So pick a pattern for that key and play the arpeggios in that pattern.

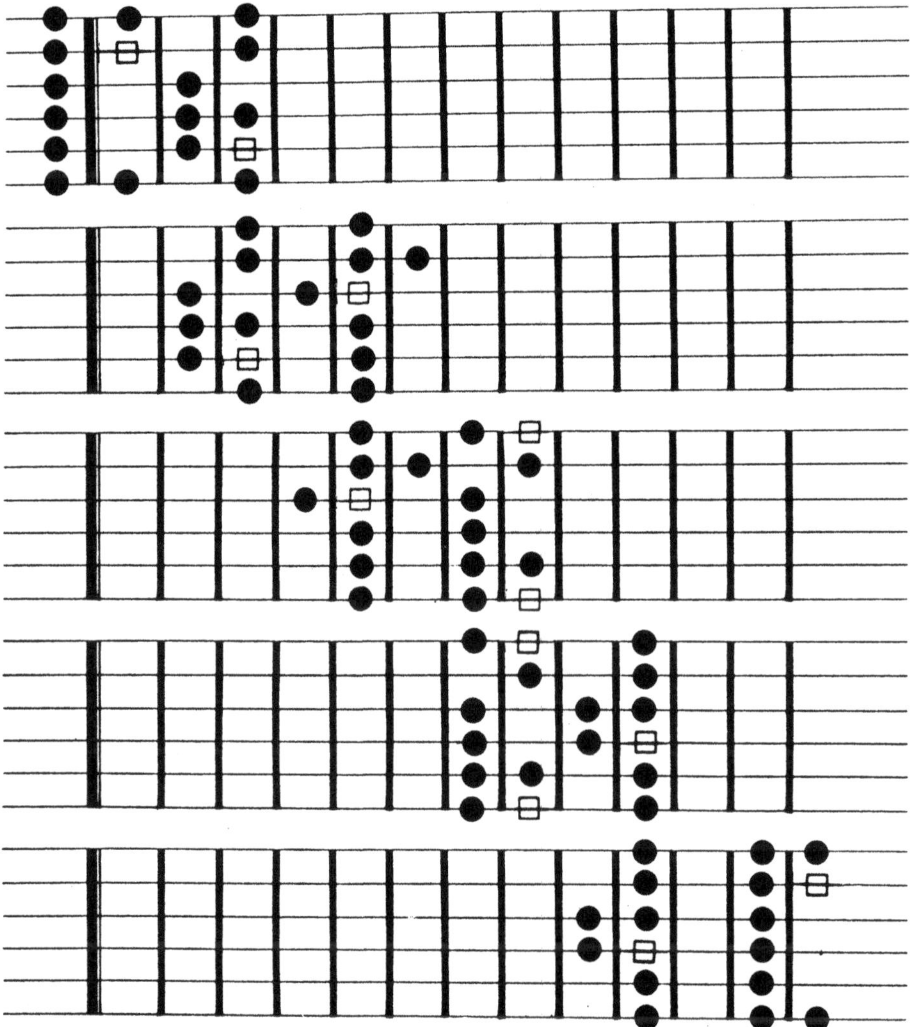

THE ZONE SYSTEM

This system comes from Duke Miller, head of the guitar department, University of Southern California. Mr Miller has fragmented the fretboard chromatically into sections or areas he coined "zones". Whereas other fretboard visualizers have dissected the fretboard diatonically (the seven diatonic pitches of the major scale alone). Duke Miller's zone system is based on all 12 chromatic pitches of western music.

The following example is the zone system.

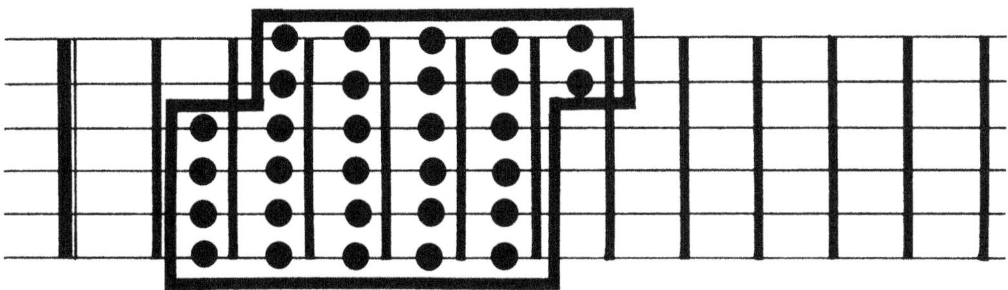

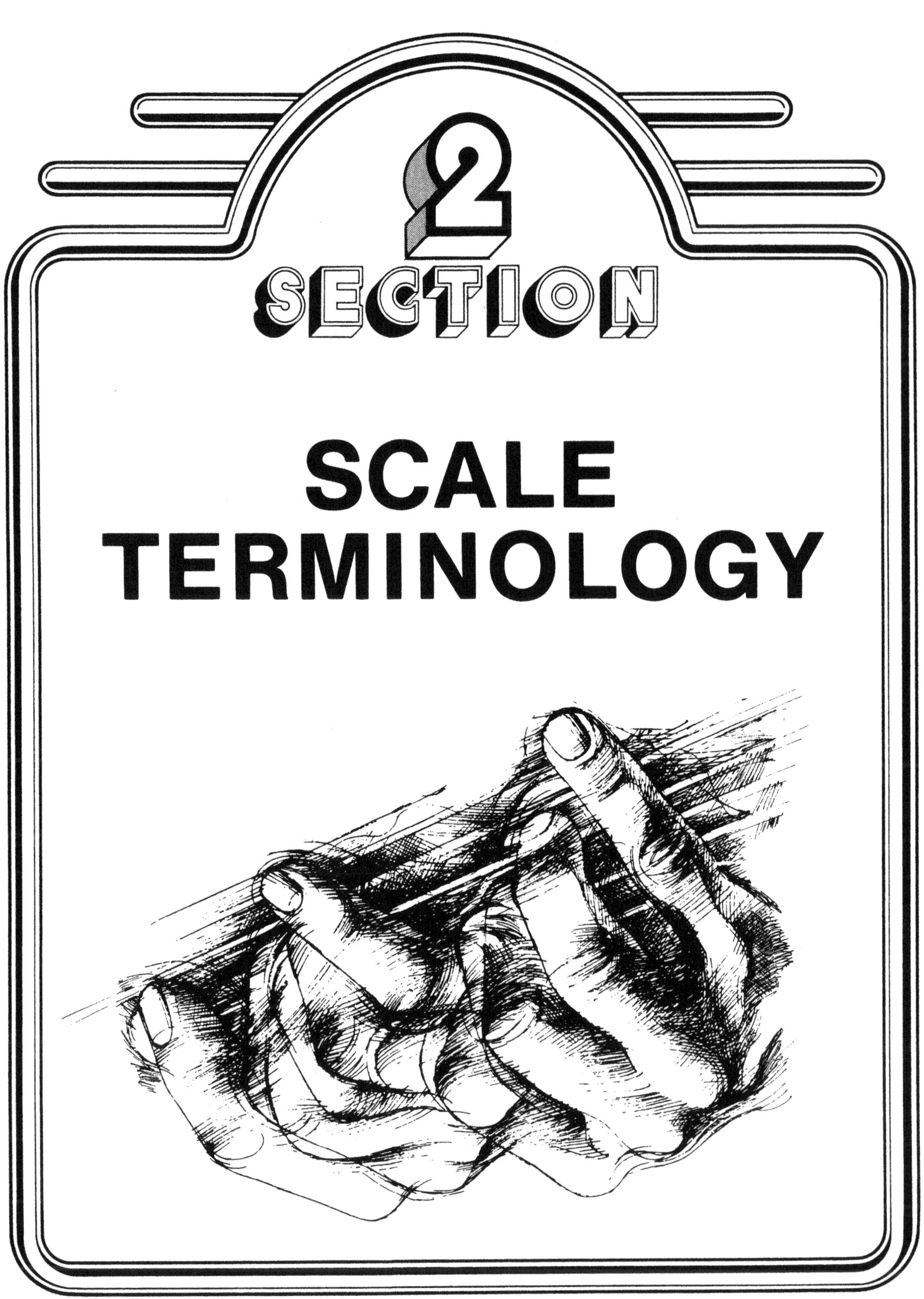

SCALE TERMINOLOGY

Whole and Half Steps
(Tones and Semitones)

The distance from one tone to the next is one half step (or semitone). This is the Chromatic Scale.

This is the chromatic scale

The distance between every other note on this scale is one whole step. One whole step equals two half steps.

This is the whole tone scale

Whole steps and half steps are the spacers that govern and regulate the construction of (most) scales and modes.

The example below is not any specific scale but a study for you to find the whole and half steps between the actual notes.

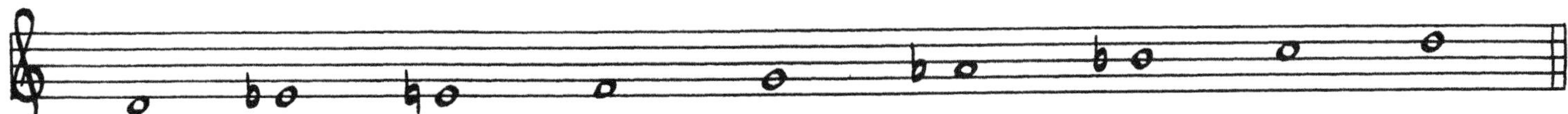

Terminology of Scale Degrees

For our general information the identifying terms of the scale degrees, using the C major scale as our example, are:

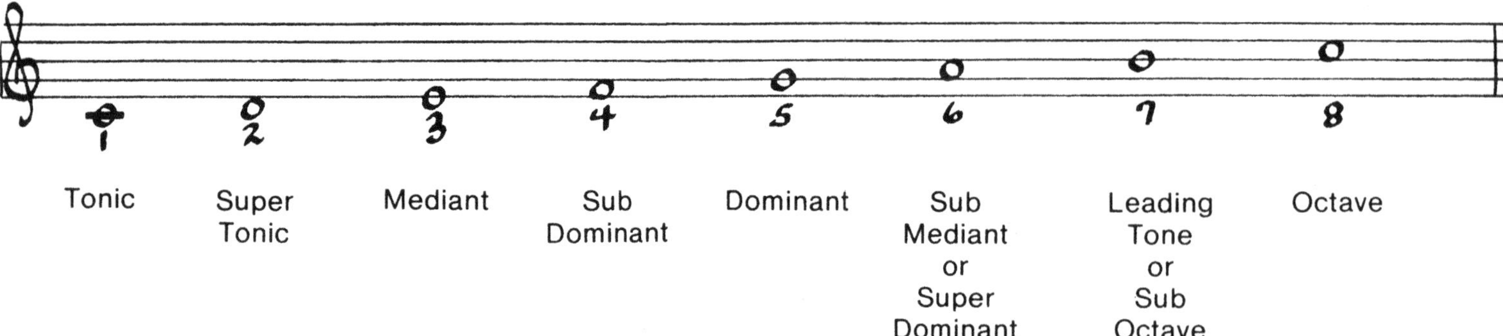

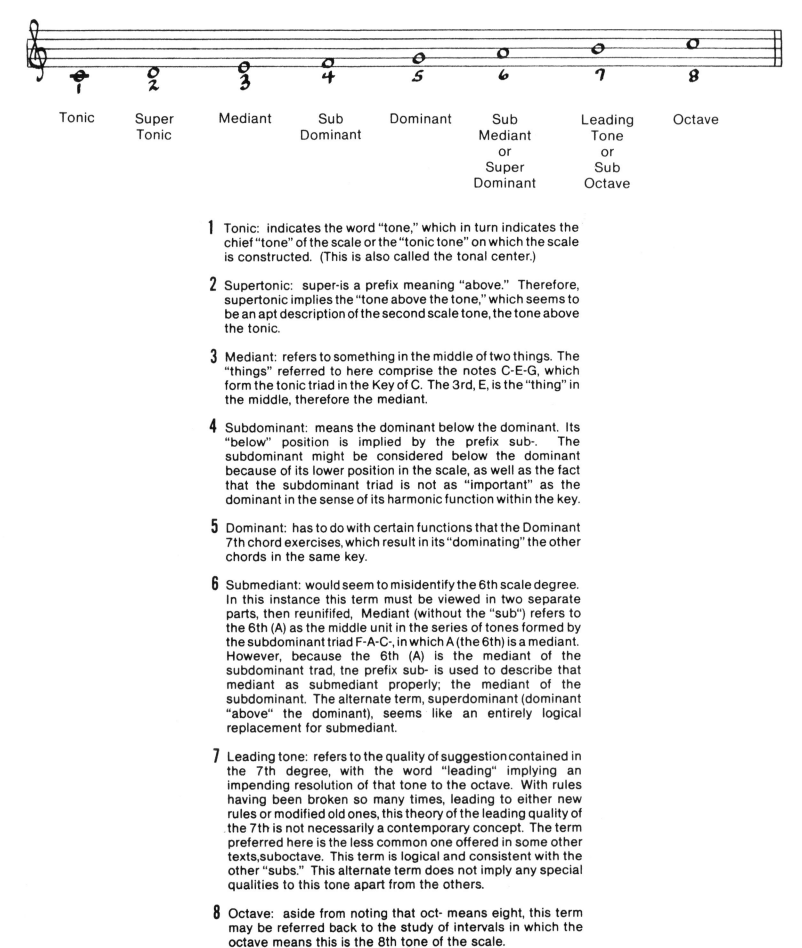

1 Tonic: indicates the word "tone," which in turn indicates the chief "tone" of the scale or the "tonic tone" on which the scale is constructed. (This is also called the tonal center.)

2 Supertonic: super-is a prefix meaning "above." Therefore, supertonic implies the "tone above the tone," which seems to be an apt description of the second scale tone, the tone above the tonic.

3 Mediant: refers to something in the middle of two things. The "things" referred to here comprise the notes C-E-G, which form the tonic triad in the Key of C. The 3rd, E, is the "thing" in the middle, therefore the mediant.

4 Subdominant: means the dominant below the dominant. Its "below" position is implied by the prefix sub-. The subdominant might be considered below the dominant because of its lower position in the scale, as well as the fact that the subdominant triad is not as "important" as the dominant in the sense of its harmonic function within the key.

5 Dominant: has to do with certain functions that the Dominant 7th chord exercises, which result in its "dominating" the other chords in the same key.

6 Submediant: would seem to misidentify the 6th scale degree. In this instance this term must be viewed in two separate parts, then reunififed, Mediant (without the "sub") refers to the 6th (A) as the middle unit in the series of tones formed by the subdominant triad F-A-C-, in which A (the 6th) is a mediant. However, because the 6th (A) is the mediant of the subdominant trad, tne prefix sub- is used to describe that mediant as submediant properly; the mediant of the subdominant. The alternate term, superdominant (dominant "above" the dominant), seems like an entirely logical replacement for submediant.

7 Leading tone: refers to the quality of suggestion contained in the 7th degree, with the word "leading" implying an impending resolution of that tone to the octave. With rules having been broken so many times, leading to either new rules or modified old ones, this theory of the leading quality of the 7th is not necessarily a contemporary concept. The term preferred here is the less common one offered in some other texts,suboctave. This term is logical and consistent with the other "subs." This alternate term does not imply any special qualities to this tone apart from the others.

8 Octave: aside from noting that oct- means eight, this term may be referred back to the study of intervals in which the octave means this is the 8th tone of the scale.

Scale Tone Intervals

An interval is the distance (or the difference in pitch) BETWEEN two notes.

The basic intervals and their identifying terms are the results of the tones of the major scales. They are identifed this way:

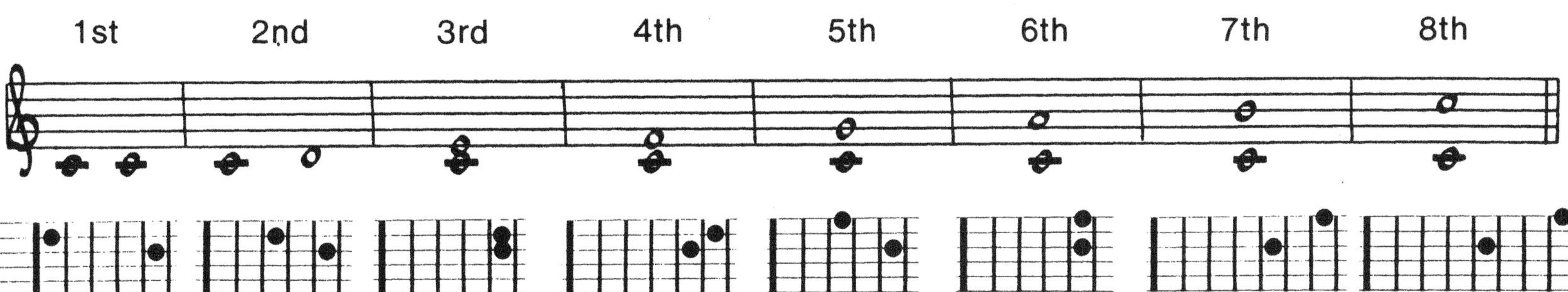

The number refers to the numerical position occupied by each tone in the scale of the lower (TONIC) tone.

The following changes make the terms more consistent with those in common use.
1.Prime replaces first (prime means first).

2.Octave replaces eight (oct means eight)

The example below shows the more common terms.

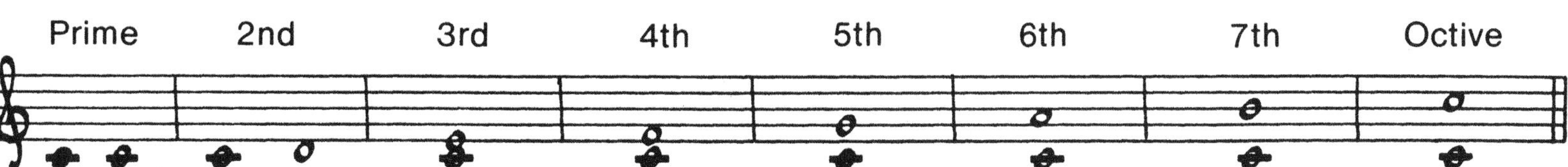

"Mastery of the BASICS is Critical"

Two Additional Terms: Perfect and Major

The perfect intervals are those involving two tones that are in each others scales. Look at that second step 'D'. While D is in the C scale, C IS NOT IN THE D SCALE. In the D scale it's C# (sharp). Then the 2nd step is called a MAJOR interval. Lets move on to the third step 'E', C is not in the E scale (in E it would be a C#). Therefore, the third step is also a major interval. Looking at the 4th step 'F'. F is in the C scale and C is in the F scale. Then the 4th is called a PERFECT INTERVAL.

Carrying it through all the scale steps the complete system of terms evolves as:

Prime-Perfect
2nd-Major
3rd-Major
4th-Perfect
5th-Perfect
6th-Major
7th-Major
8th-Perfect

The following example shows the scale tone intervals with their complete reference terms:

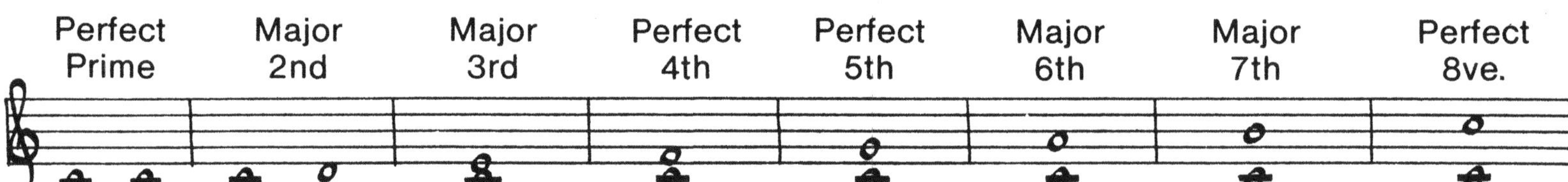

As a aid to memorizing if you divide it in half this pattern will occur:

Perfect, major, major, perfect
Perfect, major, major, perfect

Also when tones sound at the same pitch they are referred to as being in unison (meaning one sound) as in the first step.

The following are scale-tone intervals in all keys.

Basic Scale Tone Intervals In All Keys

Perfect Prime	Major 2nd	Major 3rd	Perfect 4th	Perfect 5th	Major 6th	Major 7th	Perfect Octave

C

F

Bb

Eb

Ab

Db

Gb

B

E

A

D

G

Altered Intervals

These intervals involve chromatically altered tones.

Intervals are altered in the following ways:

1. Major intervals reduced one half step become minor.
2. Perfect intervals reduced one half step become diminished.
3. Minor intervals reduced one half step become diminished.
4. Major and perfect intervals increased one half step become augmented.

The example below shows how these terms apply to altered intervals.

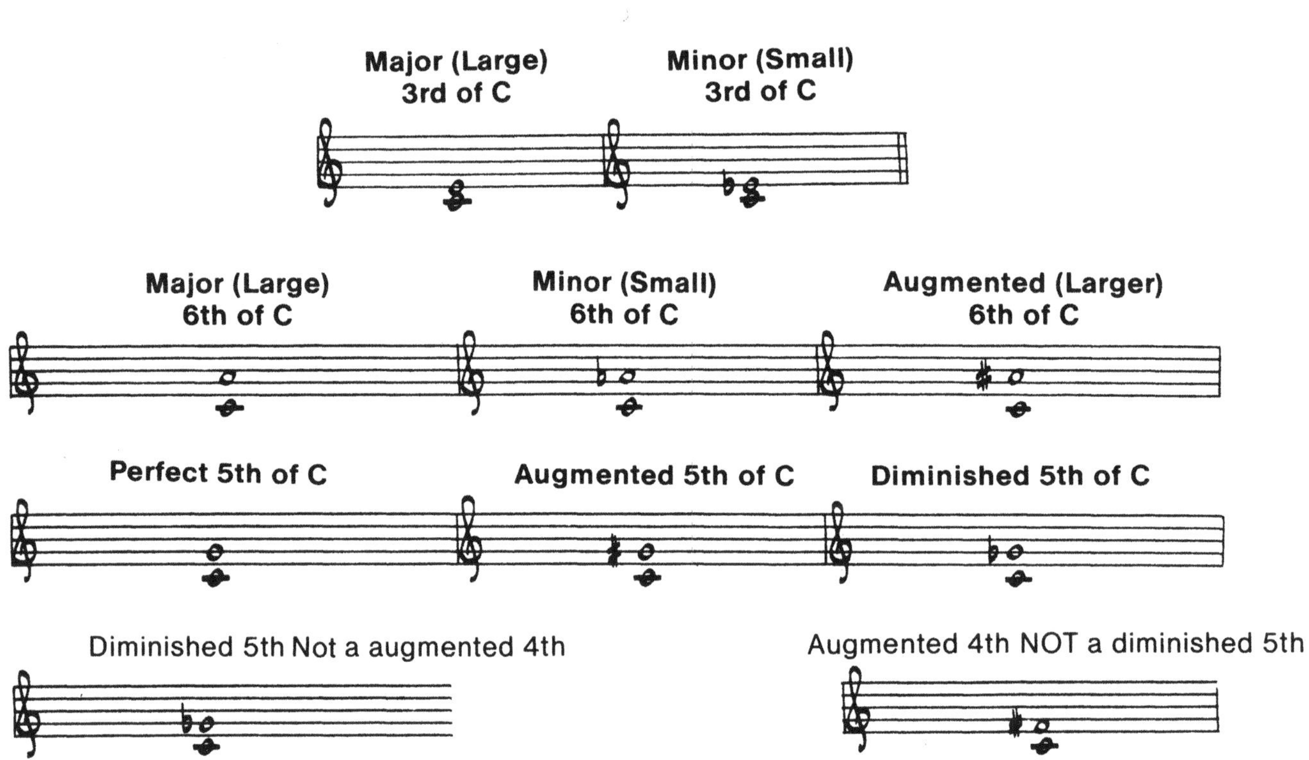

You'll notice the similarity of some intervals. For instance: the augmented 4th (C-F#) sounds the same as the diminished 5th (C-Gb). Or the minor 3rd (C-Eb) sounds like the augmented 2nd (C-D#). The augmented 5th (C-G#) is similar to the minor 6th (C-Ab) etc. Of course it makes little difference if it were just to identify the sound of the auxiliary upper tone. But using the correct name has a direct bearing on terms applied to the chords that result when specific intervals are combined. So then C to Eb shouldn't be called an augmented 2nd, because E being the third note of the scale and is lowered, it is called a minor 3rd. Likewise, it's incorrect to call C to D# the minor 3rd. D being the second note and raised one half step we call it an augmented 2nd.

All other enharmonic intervals should be carefully distinguished from one another and called by their correct scale terms. The following are altered intervals in all keys:

Altered Intervals

Maj.2 Min.2 Aug.2 Maj.3 Min.3 Aug.3 Per.4 Dim.4 Aug.4

C

F

B♭

E♭

A♭

D♭

G♭

B

E

A

D

G

	Per.5	Dim.5	Aug.5	Maj.6	Min.6	Aug.6	Maj.7	Min.7	Aug.7

C

F

B♭

E♭

A♭

D♭

G♭

B

E

A

D

G

Diminished 7th Interval in all keys

Rule:
Minor intervals reduced one half step become diminished.

The Diminished 7th does have a functional value. It is the enharmonic equivalent of the Major 6th. For example, the Diminished 7th C-B♭♭ and the Major 6th interval C-A sound alike. The two may eventually be reconciled, but for right now the Diminished 7th interval should be regarded as an individual entity.

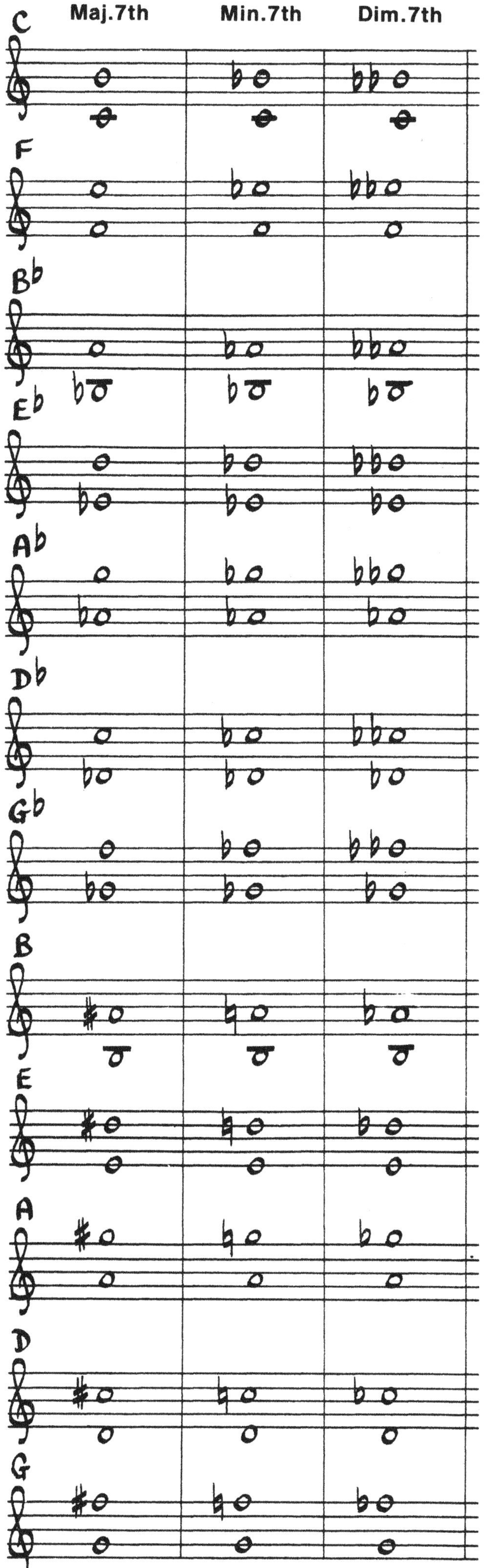

SCALES and MODES

The scales we love to hate

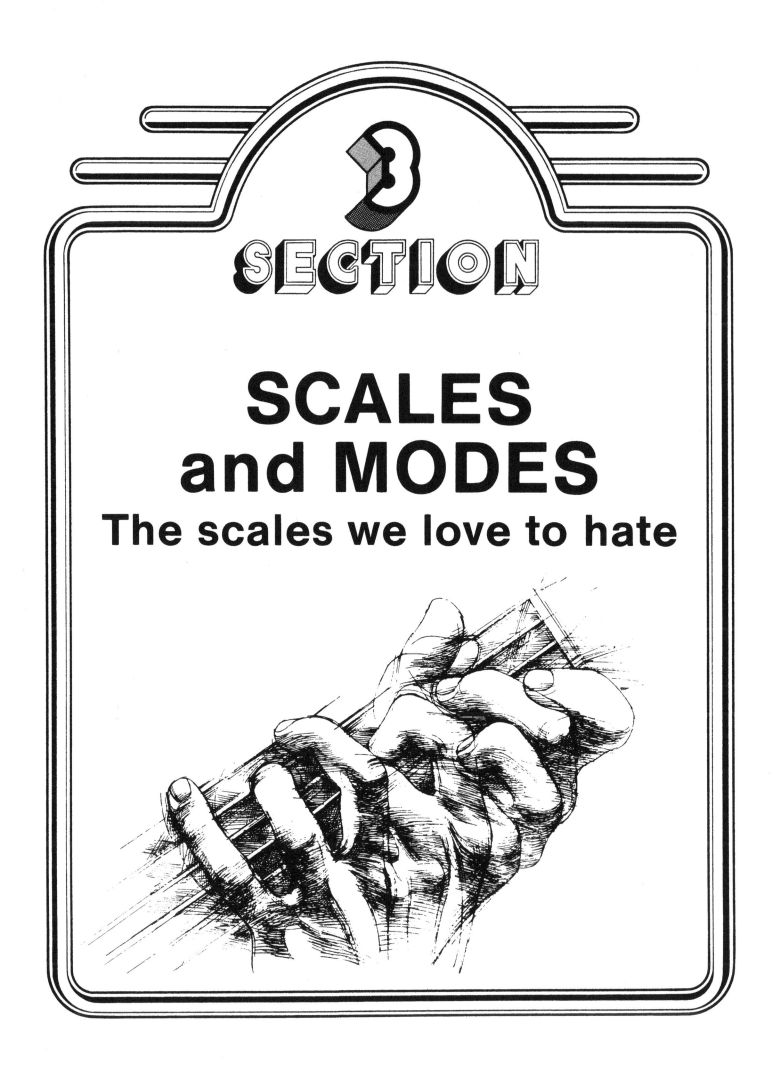

The Chromatic Scale

The chromatic scale is constructed of all half steps. There is only one chromatic scale which can begin on any tone.

Chromatic Scale

Control of the Chromatic scale is essential for building technique. Due to the fact that the guitar is a chromatic half-step instrument, (A half step equals the distance from one fret to the next). Chromatic exercises are very good for building finger independence of the fingering hand. And when played up and down the fretboard on one string helps develop our lateral movement.

Chromatic Scale in a Five-Fret Frame

Below is the Chromatic scale using Duke Miller's zone system:

Notice that the first finger slides to the next fret.

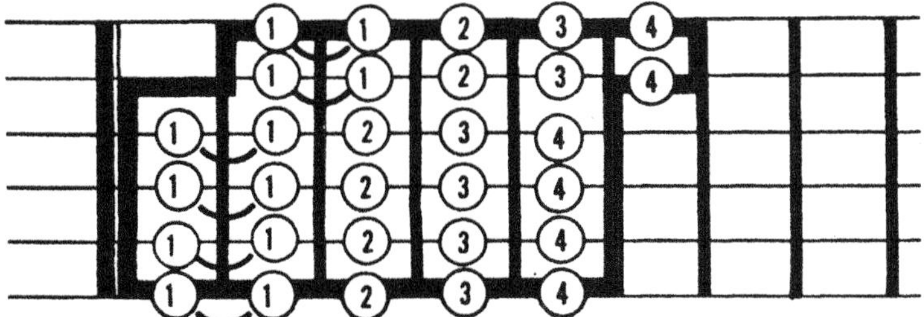

Application

The chromatic scale can be used with any chord type with any combination of alterations. Some of the scale tones will always be dissonant, (or clash) to the harmony and will have a strong tendency to move either up or down a half step to the nearest chord tone.

If used sparingly, you can create excitement in your playing. Short bursts, of say, 4 or 5 successive scale steps is all you'll need. Start out on the root, third or fifth of the chord you're playing against.

Chromatic Exercises

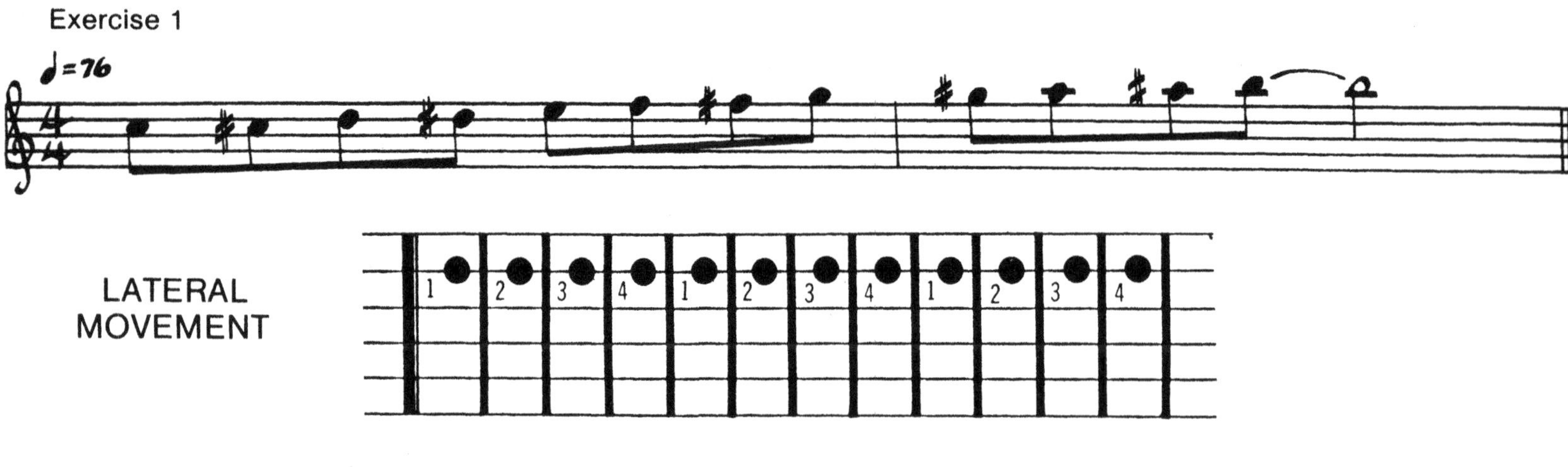

1. Played all on the second string.
2. When all four fingers have sounded, make a quick shift up the string to play the next sequence.
3. The skips must be clean and fast, no finger slides.
4. The thumb and fingers plant at the same time.
5. Play on all strings.

WHEN PLAYING A CONSECUTIVE CHROMATIC SCALE EXERCISE, LEAVE EACH FINGER DOWN AFTER IT HAS SOUNDED THE NOTE.

Exercise 2

♩=76-120

0 1 2 3 4 3 2 1 0 1 2 3 4 3 2 1

0 1 2 3 4 3 2 1 0 1 2 3 4 3 2 1

0 1 2 3 4 3 2 1 0 1 2 3 4 3 2 1

0 1 2 3 4 3 2 1 0

Exercise 3

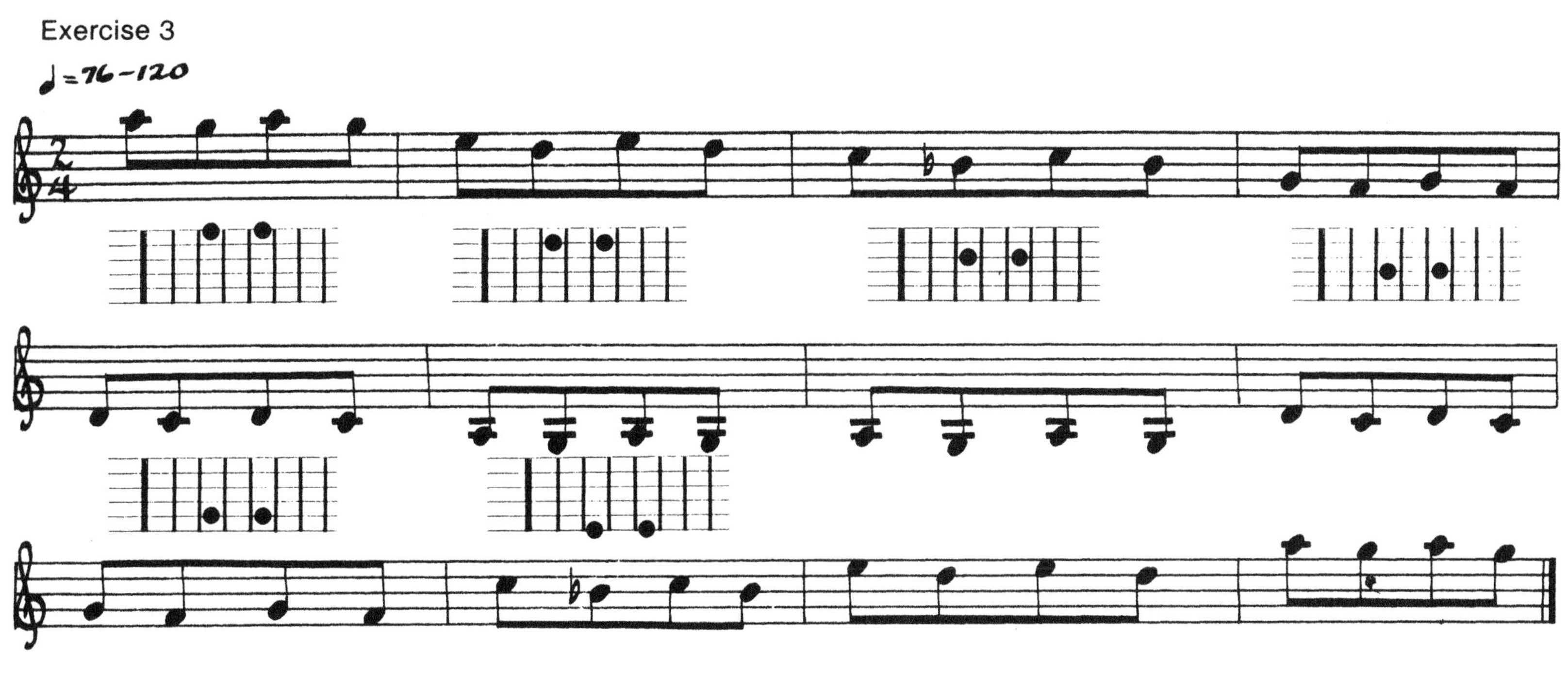

Exercise 4 Contrary motion, meaning two lines moving in different directions.

Exercise 5

Whole Tone Scale

Probably the easiest of all scales to memorize. Constructed exclusively of whole steps, 6 in all. As there are only 12 tones in the chromatic scale, then there are only two different sounding whole tone scales. Each of those two scales can be interpreted enharmonically as several different scales.

C Whole Tone

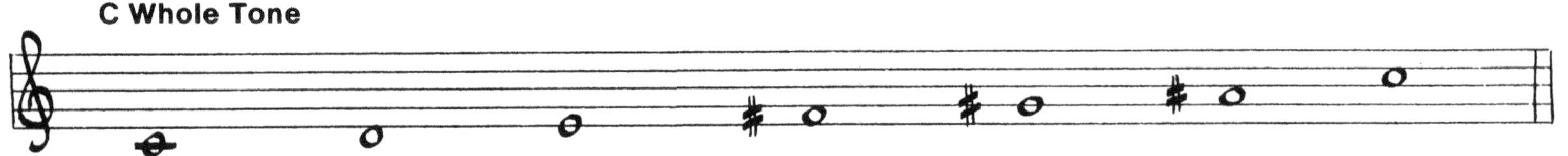

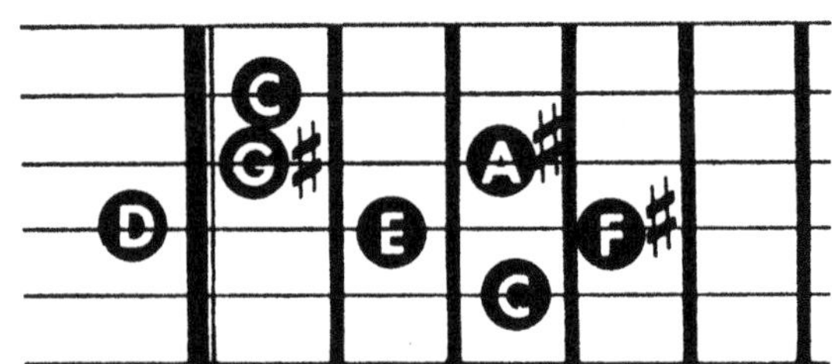

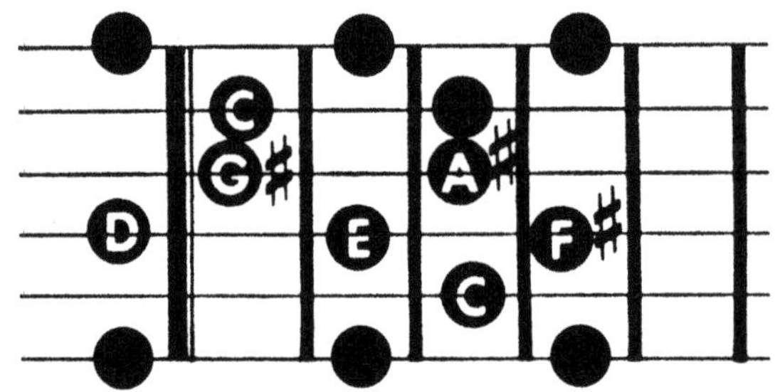

Starting with the lowest possible note in the first position.

Application

The whole tone scale, omits one letter of the musical alphabet in its spelling. Creating an interval of a Diminished 3rd between two of the scale tones.

The Diminished 3rd (same as a whole step) can occur between any two notes of the scale. This is important to remember in constructing the scale.

The whole tone scale is used with dominant family chords that have either a raised or lowered 5th or both. You'll notice that both of these alterations are present in the scale. If a lowered 5th is present, a Lydian, b7 scale (page 82) might be a better choice instead of the whole tone scale.

If an altered 9th is used in the harmony, example C7#9, the whole tone scale should not be used because of the dissonant clash with the unaltered 9th which is present in the scale.

The whole tone scale, because of it structure, is capable of generating many patterns which move up or down through the scale at some regular interval. Whole tone patterns were commonly used by many players in the Bebop era.

Exercise 1

Use the scale over the Dominant chords while improvising over these progressions:

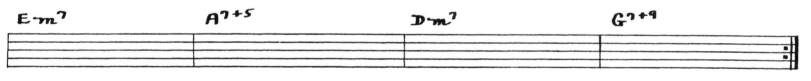

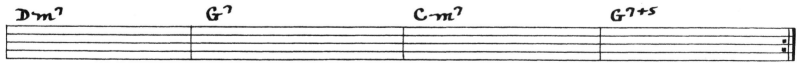

E-m7	A7+5	D-m7	G7+9
C-m7	F7	B♭ Maj.7	A7
Dm7	G7	C-m7	G7+5

Whole Tone Scales
(All Keys)

Whole Step--Half Step Diminished Scale

Constructed of 4 whole steps and 4 half-steps in regular alternation. There are only THREE different sounding diminished scales. Each one of those scales can be interpreted enharmonically as several different scales.

C Whole step-Half step Diminished

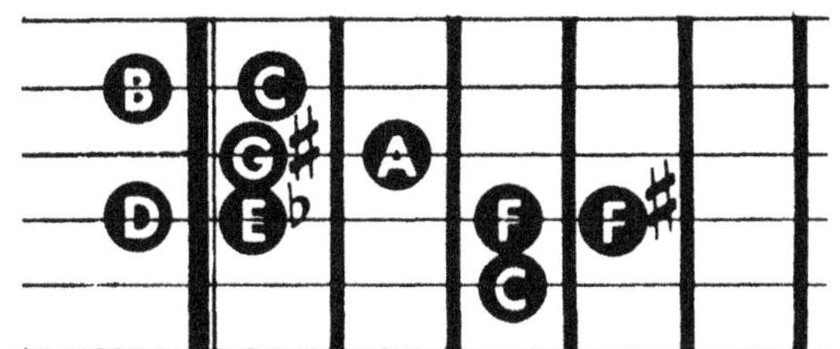

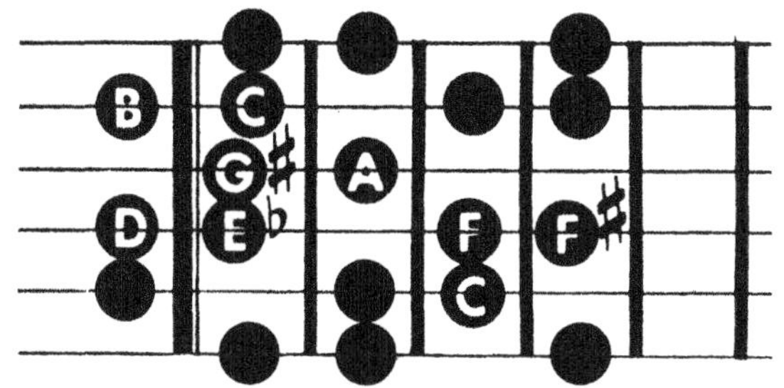

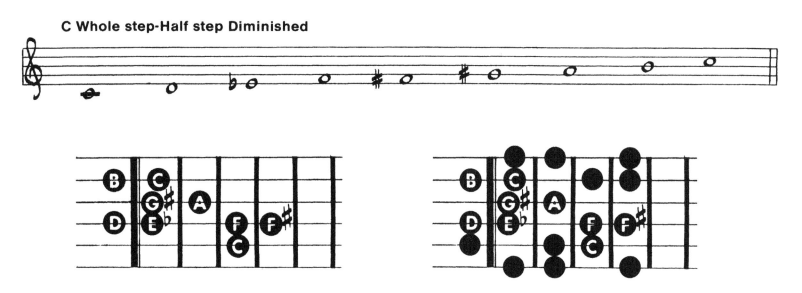

Application

The whole step-half step Diminished scale is used with the DIMINISHED 7th CHORD. The scale having only 8 tones. 4 of the tones of the Diminished 7th chord are found within the scale and 4 tones which are found a whole step above the tones of the chord. These are the notes that are most added to a Dim.7 chord to add color or to fill it out.
Any note of the scale may be emphasized or leaned on as all notes will sound acceptable with a Diminished 7th chord.

Diminished scale patterns are commonly used today. The scale is capable of creating many patterns that move up or down through the scale at some regular interval.

This scale can also be used with a half-diminished chord that leads to a dominant chord a 5th below. (Example: C7Dim to F7). Some notes will clash and sound off but this soon disappears as the chord changes.

The easy thing to remember is that beginning with a whole step we can construct it on the root of the chord it accompanies.

Lastly this scale is really the same as the half-whole diminished scale only starting on a different note.

Whole Step-Half Step Diminished Scales

Half Step--Whole Step Diminished Scale

This scale is constructed of 4 half steps and 4 whole steps in regular alternation. There are only THREE DIFFERENT sounding diminished scales. Each one of those scales can be interpreted enharmonically as several different scales.

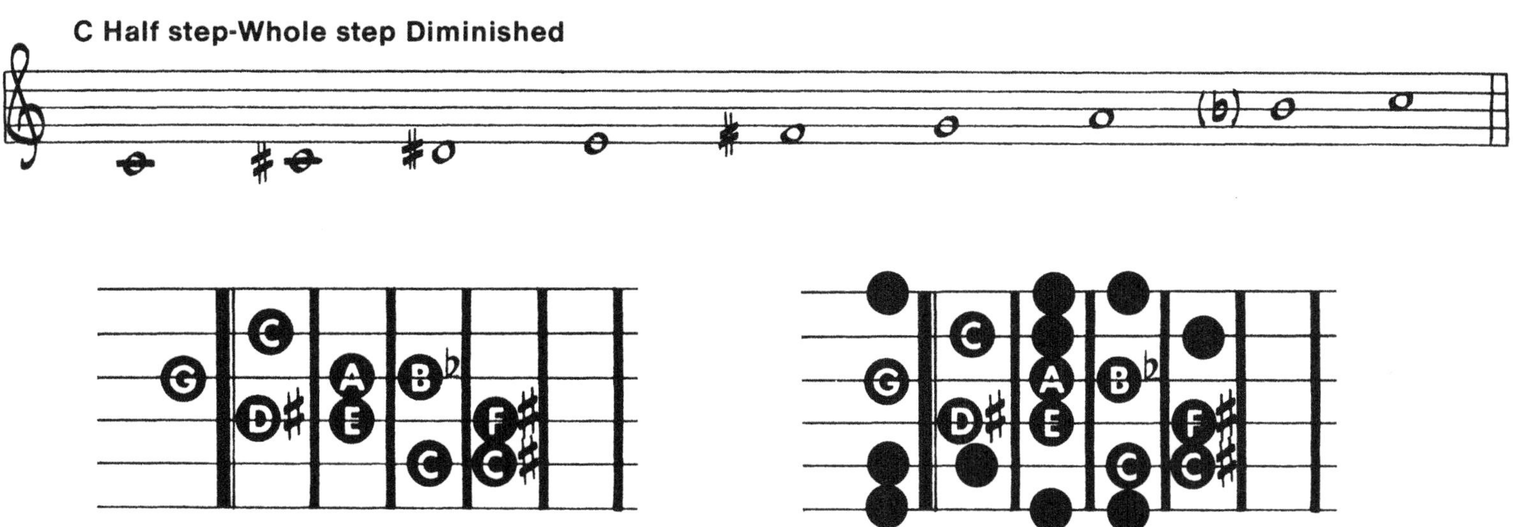

Application

The half step-whole step Diminished scale is used with a Dominant 7th family chord. That has wither a raised or lowered 9th or both present. Using C7#9 chord as an example, you'll notice that both the raised 9th (D#) and the lowered 9th (D♭) are present in the scale. The other scale tones are the root, 3rd, 5th, b7th, #11th and 13th.

If a raised 5th is present in the harmony the diminished scale should not be used because of the dissonant clash with the unaltered 5th that's in the scale. If a lowered 5th is present in the chord, the diminished scale could be used, but a better choice might be the Super Locrian.

Diminished scale patterns are commonly used today. The scale is capable of creating many patterns that move up anbd down through the scale at some regular interval.

Lastly, this scale is really the same as the whole-half diminished scale only starting on a different note.

The easy thing to remember is that beginning with a half step we can construct it on the root of the chord it accompanies.

Half Step-Whole Step Diminished Scales

Augmented Scale

This scale is constructed of 3 half steps and 3 intervals of a minor 3rd (augmented 2nd). The minor 3rds occur in regular alternation with the half steps. There are only FOUR DIFFERENT sounding augmented scales. Each of these scales can be interpreted enharmonically as several different scales.

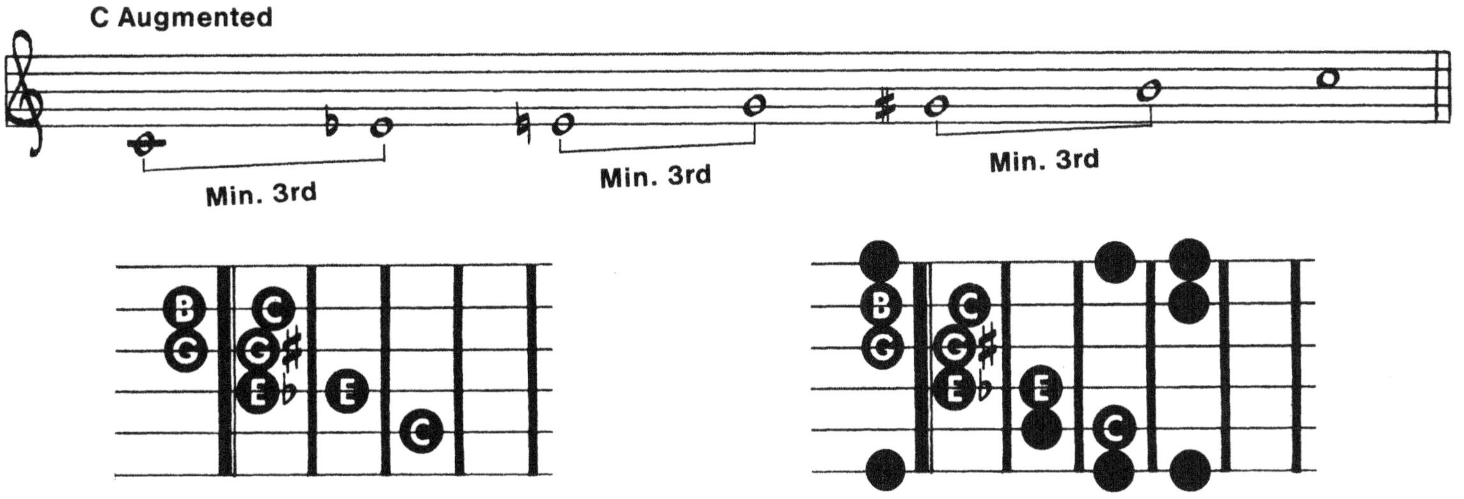

Using the lowest note in the first position.

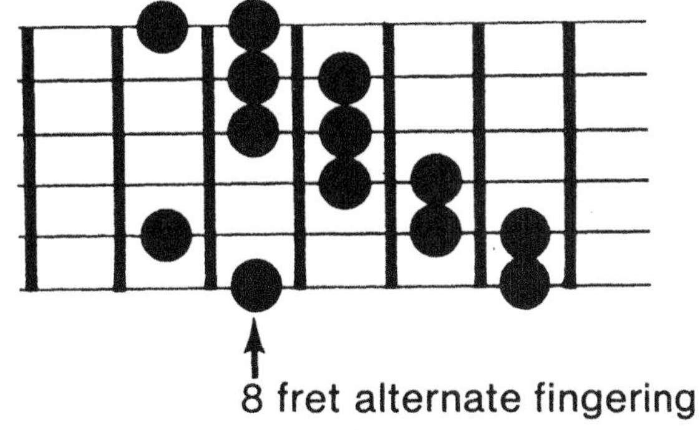

Application

The Augmented scale is used with major family chords that have a raised 5th present in the harmony. There are actually six augmented triads, the roots of which form two augmented triads, in the scale. There are also three major triads present in the scale.

The Augmented scale, because of its symmetry can create patterns that move up or down through the scale at some regular interval. These are less common than whole tone or diminished patterns but sound very effective.

Augmented Scales

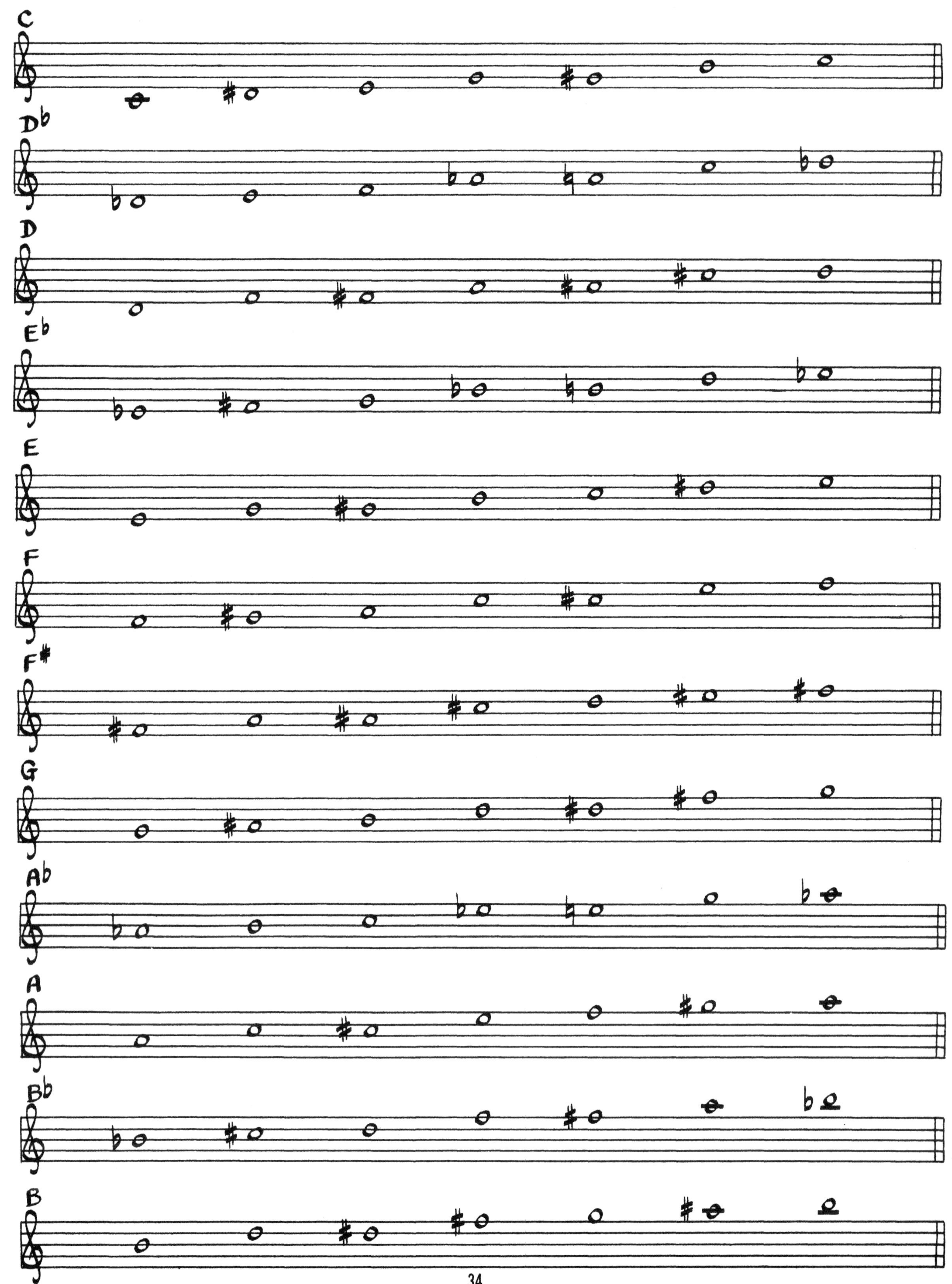

Modes Generated by the Major Scale

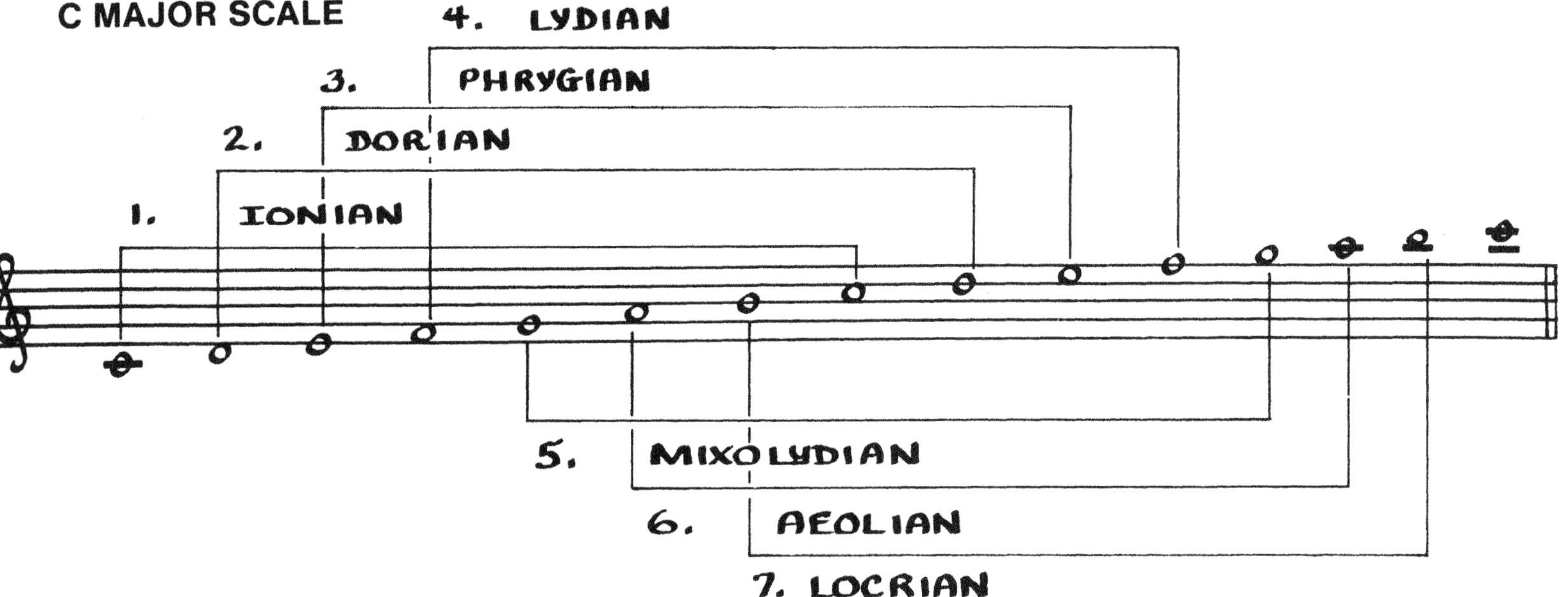

A mode is formed simply by taking a scale, such as the 'C' Major scale, and instead of starting on the note C, you start from any other note in the scale and play up to the SAME note an octave higher.

1. C to C, Ionian (major)–Ī-ṓ-nē-an

2. D to D, Dorian–Dōr′-ē-an

3. E to E, Phrygian–Frig′-e-an

4. F to F, Lydian–Lyd′-ē-an

5. G to G, Mixolydian–Mix-ō-lyd′-ē-an

6. A to A, Aeolian (pure minor)–Ē-ṓ-le-an

7. B to B, Locrian–Lō-cri-an

For a more in depth study of the modes look for my book 'Scale Power' Published by CENTERSTREAM.

The Major (Ionian) Scale

Constructed of 5 whole steps and 2 half steps. The half steps occur between steps 3 and 4 and steps 7 and 8 of the scale.

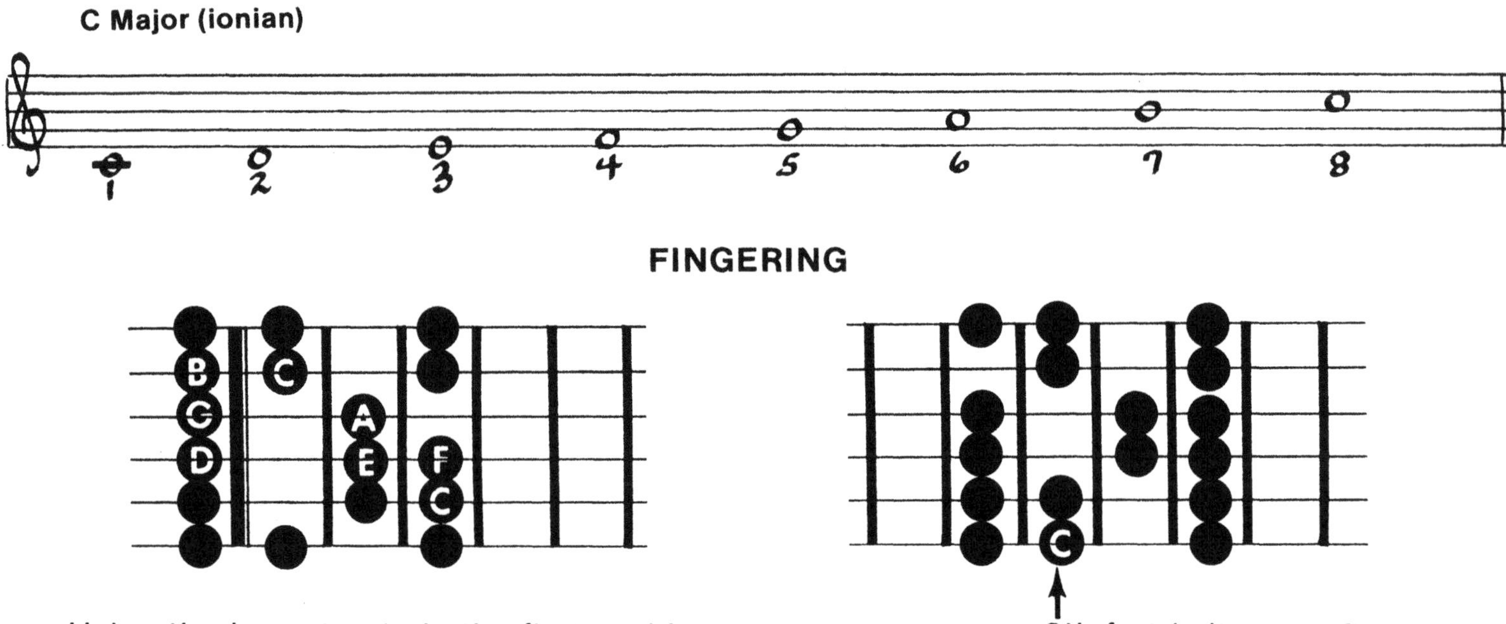

Using the lowest note in the first position.

8th fret (alternate fingering)

Application

The Major scale is used with major family chords. i.e. major triad, major 7th and major 6th-9th chords. The scale shouldn't be used when a note not in the scale ispresent in the harmony (example #5 or #11,b9 etc.) Other scales are better suited for these.

The 4th scale step is dissonant to a major chord. It has a strong tendency to resolve to the 3rd of the chord. Also if the major 7th is in the chord (like Cmaj7) the 1st or 8th scale step is relatively dissonant. It has a tendency to "resolve" or go back to the 7th.

The strong notes of the scale are the 1 (if a major 7th is not used) 2, 3, 5, 6, and 7 steps. Note that the 2, 3, 5, 6, and 7 steps form a minor pentatonic scale constructed on the 3rd of a major chord.

Major (Ionian) Scales

Dorian Mode

The Dorian scale is constructed of 5 whole steps and 2 half steps. The half steps occure between steps 2 and 3 and steps 6 and 7 of the scale.

D Dorian

FINGERING

Since this scale resides in the major scale the fingering should be of no difficulty. Your fingers already know it. Lets take the all famillar C Major scale just change the tonic or root to make a D Dorian.

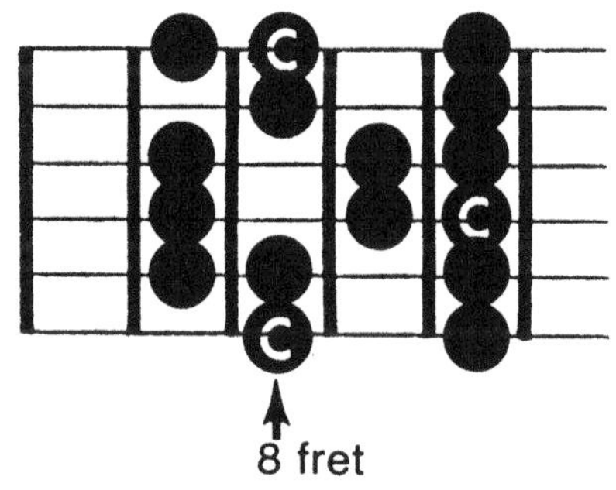

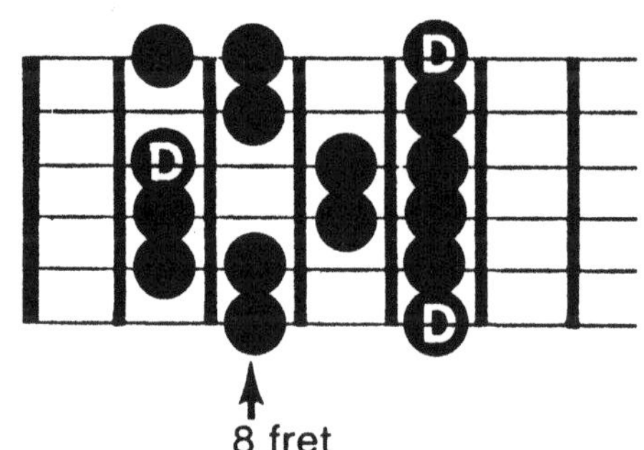

Three ways of conceiving a Dorian scale:

1. A pure minor scale with a raised 6th scale step.
2. A major scale with lowered 3rd and 7th scale steps.
3. A scale having the same key signature as the major scale a whole step below. (D Dorian has the key signature of C Major).

Application

Used with minor family chords that do not have any alterations. For example, the Dorian C m scale can be used over the II, V, change. (Cm7 to F13) And try using it over the Dominant 7th chord (same root) C7#9 to produce a blues sound.

The Dorian minor differs from the natural (relative) minor by the location of the upper half-step. In the natural minor it occurs between the 5th and 6th steps. In the Dorian the half steps are between the 6th and 7th steps.

Play the scale over the progression below:

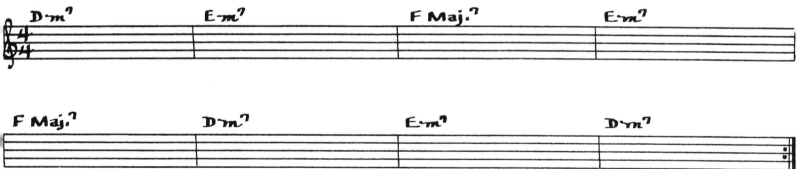

Dm7	Em7	F Maj.7	Em7
F Maj.7	Dm7	Em7	Dm7

Since the Dorian scale is so widely used today, On the following page are 10 different fingerings and patterns to play the C Dorian to get you to use the whole fretboard and just maybe to stimulate your imagination. Of course, they should be played in all keys.

8th Fret
6
5
4
5
6
8th Fret
6
5
4
5
6
8th Fret
6
5
4
3
4
5
6
3rd Fret
5
4
3
4
5
3rd Fret
5
4
3
4
5
12th Fret
5
4
3
2
3
4
5
10th Fret
4
3
2
3
4
10th Fret
4
3
2
3
4
10 Fret
4
3
2
1
2
3
4
5th Fret
3
2
1
2
3

Dorian Scales

Phrygian Mode

The Phrygian Mode is constructed of 5 whole steps and 2 half steps. The half steps occur between 1 and 2 and steps 5 and 6 of the scale.

rygian

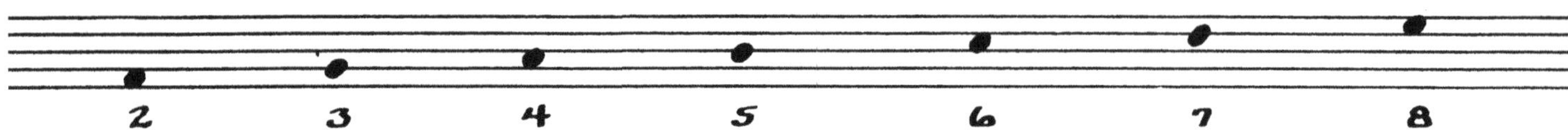

FINGERING

The fingering again should be no real problem, using the C major scale just change the tonic making it an E Phrygian.

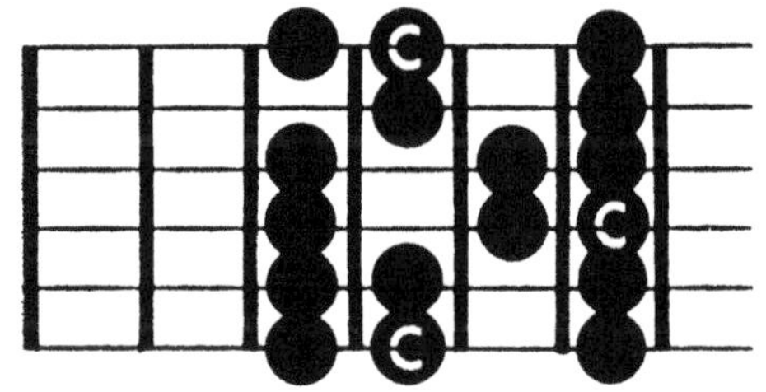

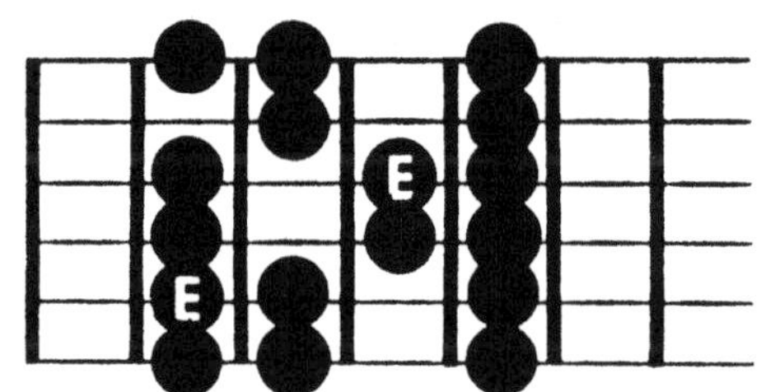

Two ways of conceiving a Phrygian mode:

1. A pure minor scale with a lowered 2nd scale step.

E MINOR: E F# G A B C D E

E PHRYGIAN: E F G A B C D E

2. A scale having the same key located a major 3rd below (E phrygian has the same key signature as C Major).

Application

This scale can be applied to minor keys, or to momentary key centers, in which the II chord is a major 7th chord. Located one half-step above the tonic minor 7th.

In the progression below, the E phrygian scale can be used throughout since the II chord, Fmaj.7 is one half-step above the tonic minor chord Em7.

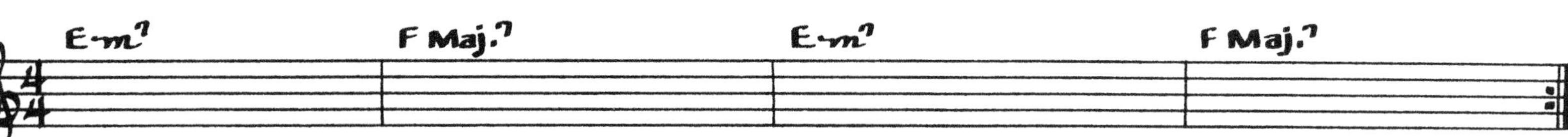

Other progressions where you could use the phrygian mode over:

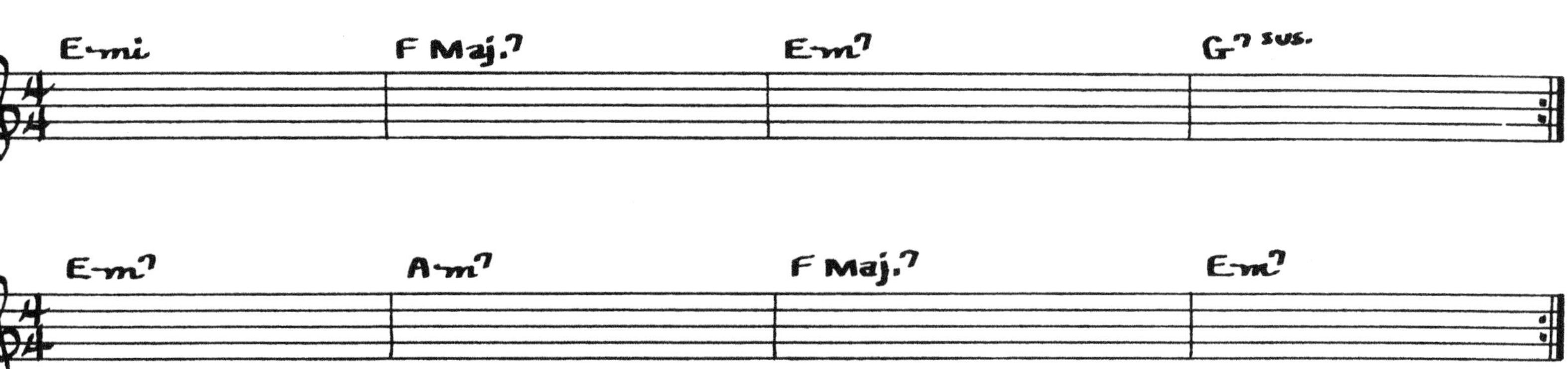

"The musician who knows his instrument well, will have a much better chance of unlocking the music that is locked within his brain".

Phrygian Scales

Lydian Mode

Constructed of 5 whole steps and 2 half steps. The half steps occur between steps 4 and 5 and steps 7 and 8 of the mode.

F Lydian

FINGERING

The fingering again should be no real problem, using the C major scale just change the tonic making it an F Lydian.

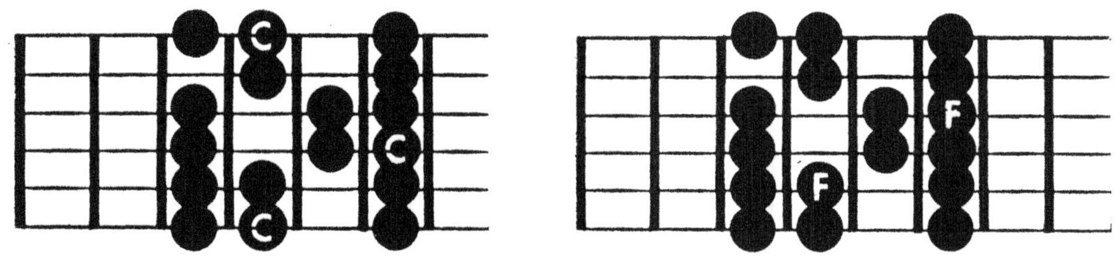

Two ways of conceiving a LYDIAN mode:

1. A major scale with a raised 4th scale step.

F MAJOR   F G A B♭ C D E F
F LYDIAN   F G A B C D E F

2. A scale having the same key signature as the major scale located a perfect 4th below (F Lydian has the same key signature as C major).

Application

The Lydian mode is used major family chords. The 1st step may be fairly dissonant when the major 7th is present (F maj.7), It wants to resolve down to the 7th. All the notes of the mode are strong. Note: That we also have the minor pentatonic scale here, The 3rd, 5th,6th 7th and 2nd steps.

Lydian Scales

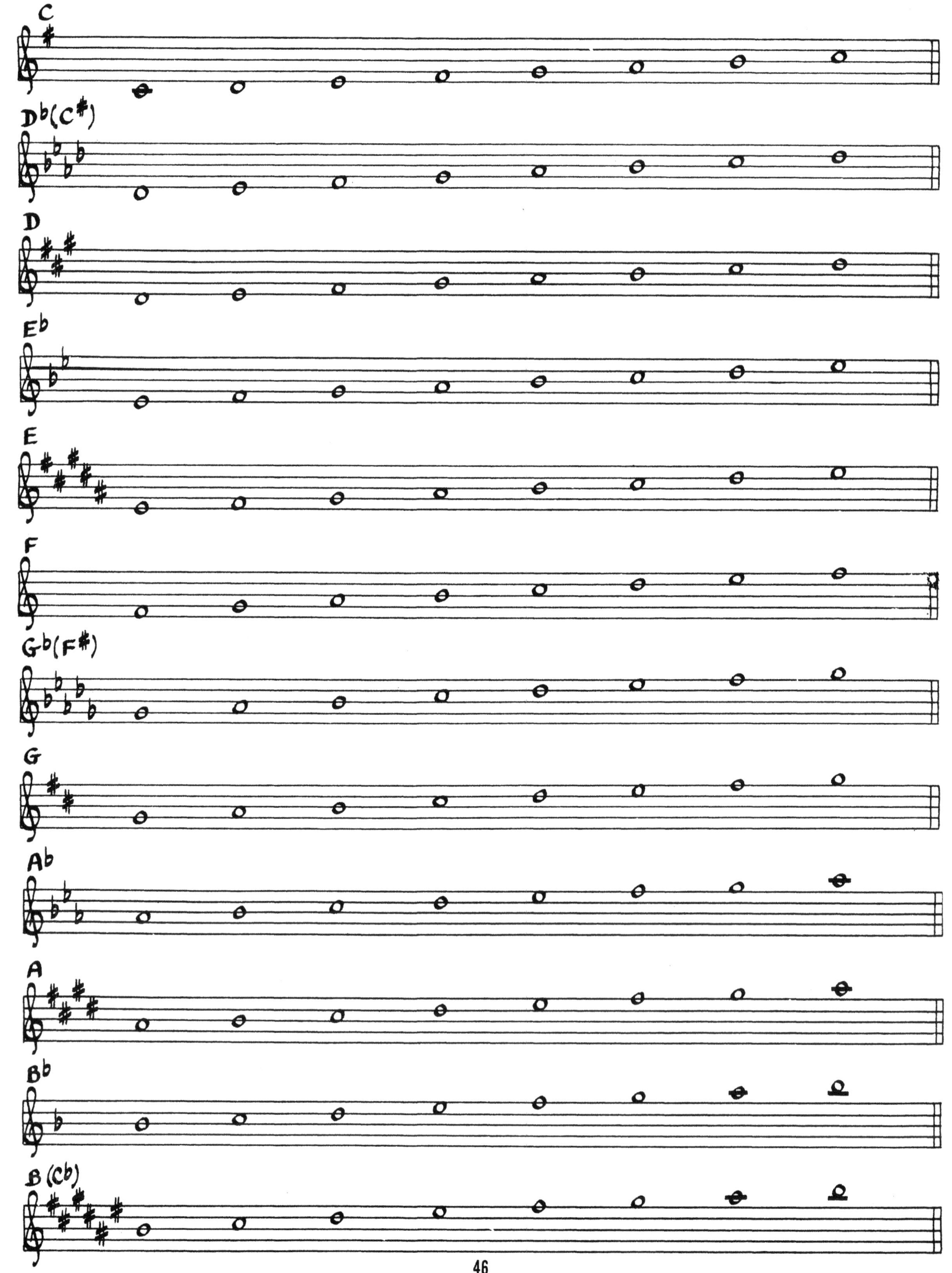

Mixolydian Mode

Constructed of 5 whole steps and 2 half steps. The half steps occur between steps 3 and 4 and steps 6 and 7 of the mode.

G Mixolydian

FINGERING

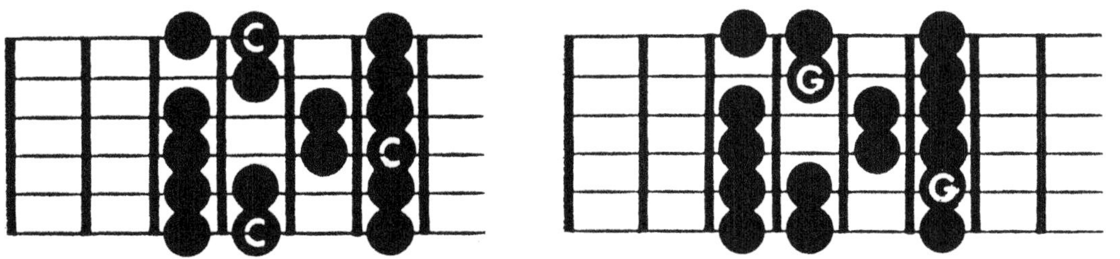

Two ways of conceiving a Mixolydian mode:

1. A major scale with a lowered 7th scale step.

G MAJOR	G A B C D E F♯ G
G MIXOLYDIAN	G A B C D E F G

2. A scale having the same key signature as the major scale located a perfect 4th above (G Mixolydian has the same key signature as C major).

Application

Sometimes called the dominant scale, the Mixolydian is used with dominant family harmonies where no alterations are present such as G7b5, G7#9,G7#5, etc.

The 4th step (C) is dissonant to a dominant 7th chord (D7). It wants to resolve back to the 3rd of the chord, but if used gives a 'bluesy' feel to it. The Mixolydian can be used if a suspended 4th is present (G7sus.4). In this case the 4th step is strong rather than the 3rd, The 7th step is also good strong one to lean on.

Mixolydian (Dominant) Scales

Aeolian Mode

(Pure Minor)
(Relative Minor)
(The Natural Minor)

A scale of many names, constructed of 5 whole steps and 2 half steps. The half steps occure between steps 2 and 3 and steps 5 and 6.

A Aeolian

FINGERING

If you know the fingerings for the major scales, you already know them for the minors. Just change the tonic or root in your mind.

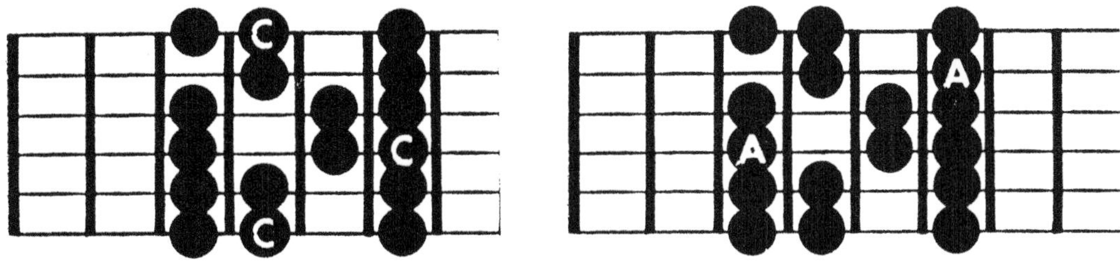

This is the mode that results from playing the major scale STARTING ON THE SIXTH SCALE STEP (in the key of C) start on the 'A' note and begin the new scale at that point.

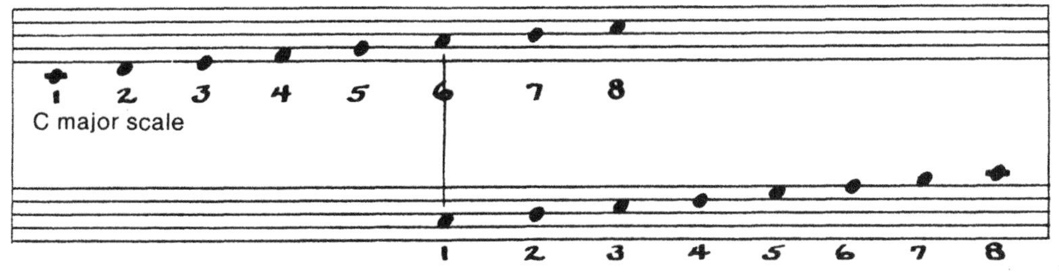

Application

The Natural Minor Scale can be used over minor harmony where the new tonic chord 1m7 is the old V1m7 of the major key. Where the major and minor keys go together in this manner are called RELATIVE KEYS.

Key of C Major---Am, Relative Key
Key of D Major---Bm, Relative Key
Key of E Major---C#m, Relative Key
Key of F Major---Dm, Relative Key
Key of G Major---Em, Relative Key
Key of A Major---F#m, Relative Key

The natural minor scale is best used on the chord built on the second step of the minor key. That chord is a minor 7th with a LOWERED 5TH (m7b5)
If you run across a progression such as the one below. The tip off is the m7b5 chord. You'll know the natural minor scale is the one to use.

Play the D Natural minor over the progression below.

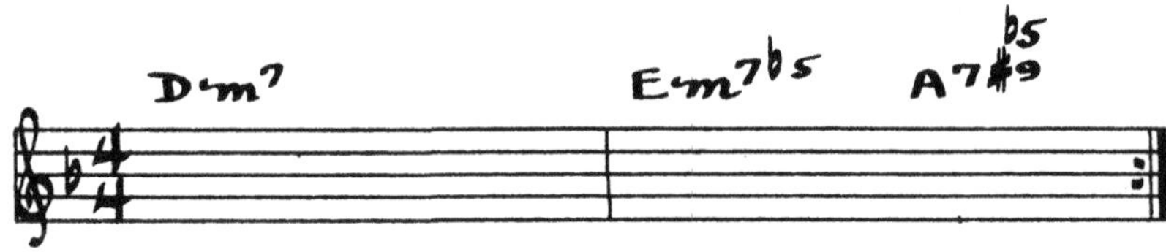

What natural minor scale would you use over this progression:

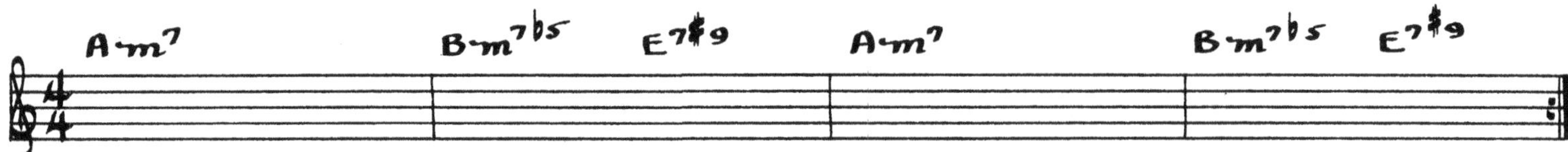

Aeolian (Pure Minor) Scales

Locrian Mode

Constructed of 5 whole steps and 2 half steps. The half steps occur between steps 1 and 2 and steps 4 and 5 of the mode.

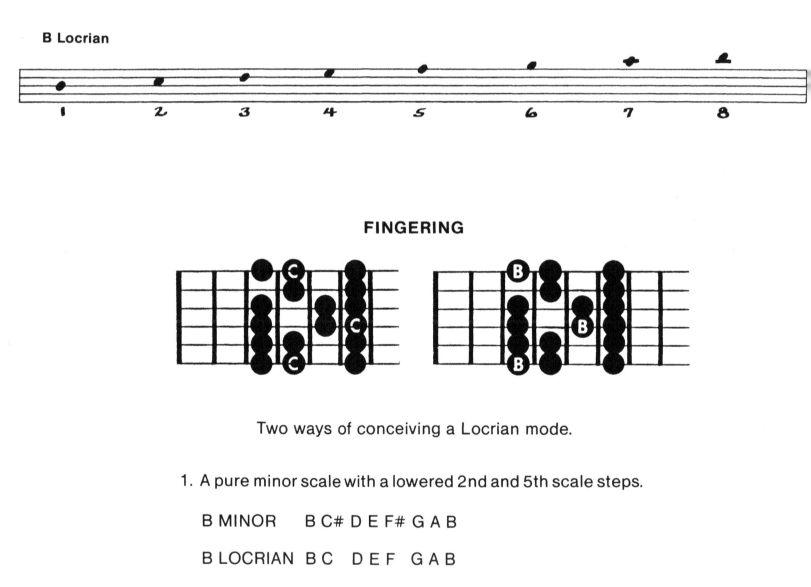

B Locrian

FINGERING

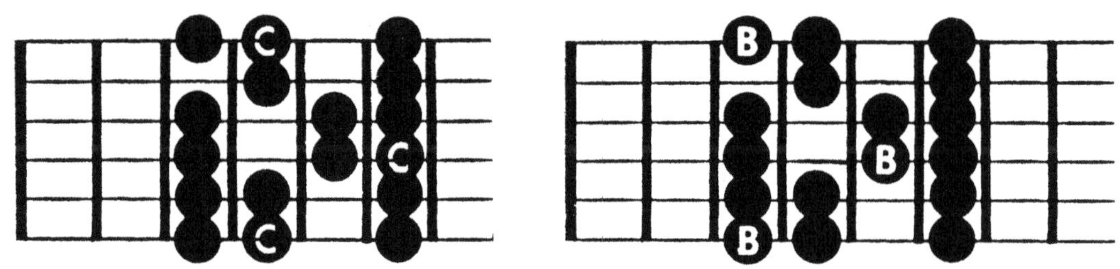

Two ways of conceiving a Locrian mode.

1. A pure minor scale with a lowered 2nd and 5th scale steps.

   B MINOR B C# D E F# G A B

   B LOCRIAN B C D E F G A B

2. Sometimes called the half-diminished mode, It's used with minor 7th chords that have a lowered 5th (Bm7b5).

Application

The 2nd scale step is dissonant, it wants to resolve to the root or 1st scale step of the chord. If the Locrian mode is used with a half diminished chord that has the unaltered 9th in it, the 2nd scale step must be raised to a half step to avoid a dissonant clash with the harmony.

Locrian Scales

Pentatonic Scales

The Pentatonic scales are probably the most popular scales used by beginning guitarest today. The scale can blend with many types of chords, i.e.; major 7, minor 7 and dominant 7th chords. And can easily function in Rock, Blues, Country, Jazz, Latin, almost any context. Plus the visual patterns are easily memorized.

In short, it'a a hard scale to get in trouble with.

This scale has been around probably as long as the guitar itself, occuring in the music of many cultures of the world, including Chinese, Polynesian, American Indian, African, Scottish Celtic and in many Gregorian chants.

The Pentatonic scales are five note scales made up of major seconds and minor thirds and having no leading tone (seventh scale degree of a major scale). And no half steps make THESE SCALES INVERTIBLE. One way is to think of it as a major scale with no fourth and seventh scale steps.

C Major Pentatonic

It can be seen that each pentatonic has five possible inverisons we call modes.

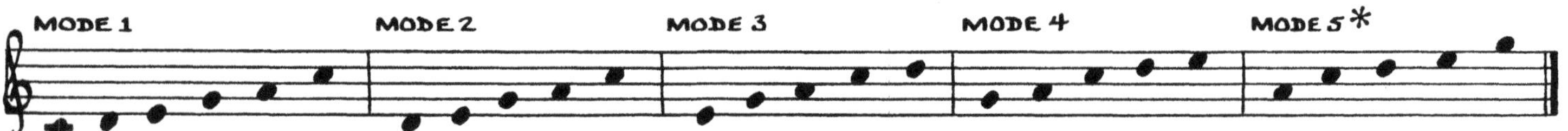

*Sometimes called the blue Pentatonic scale.

Pentatonic fingering

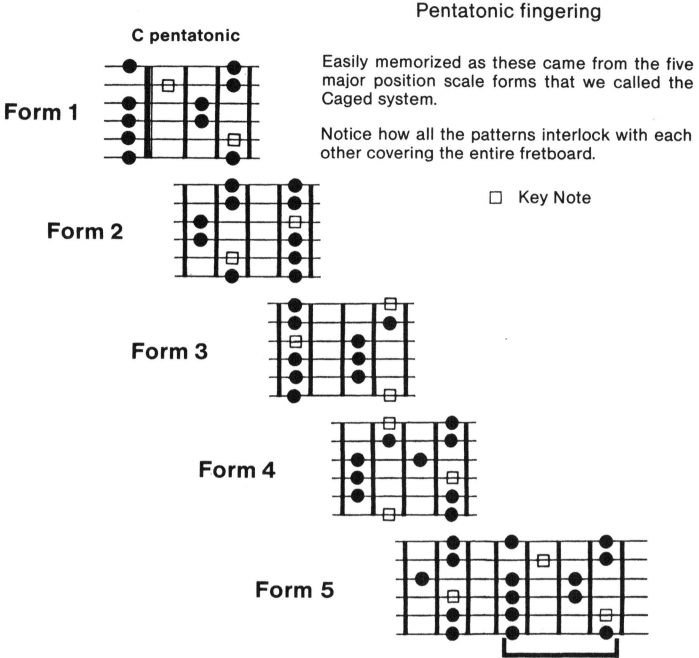

C pentatonic

Form 1

Easily memorized as these came from the five major position scale forms that we called the Caged system.

Notice how all the patterns interlock with each other covering the entire fretboard.

□ Key Note

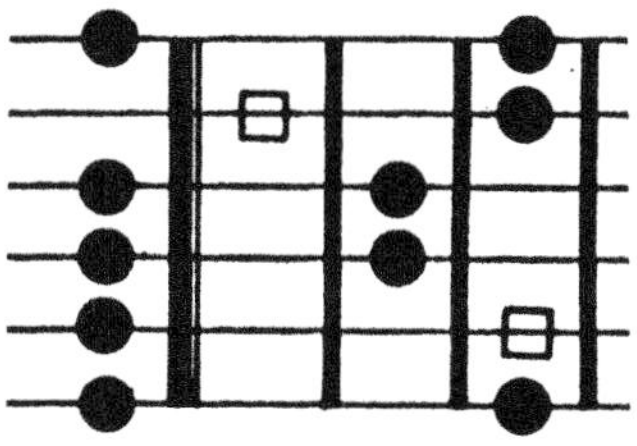

Form 2

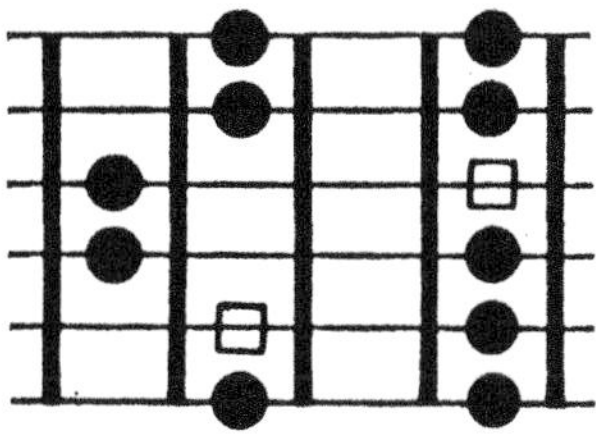

Form 3

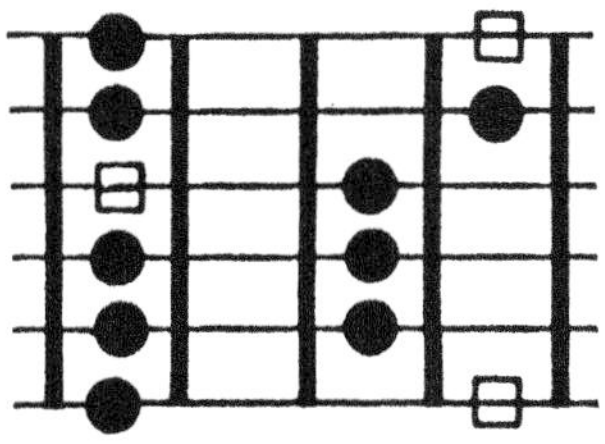

Form 4

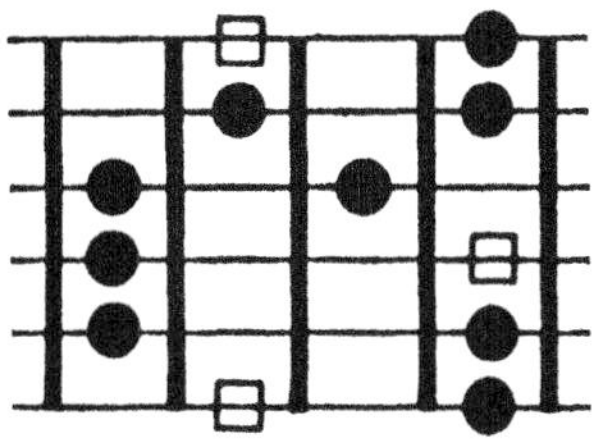

Form 5

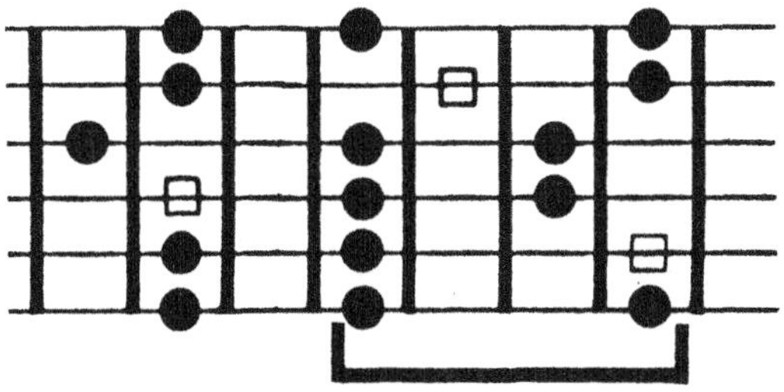

Same as the first form or pattern.

Below are some good licks used in Rock, Country or Jazz. Play them up and down the fretboard.

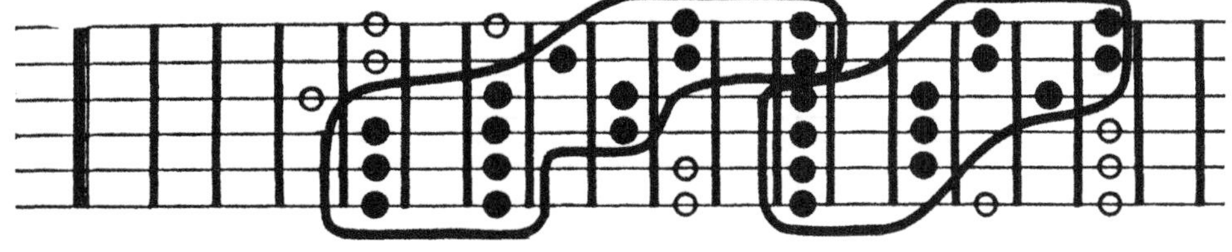

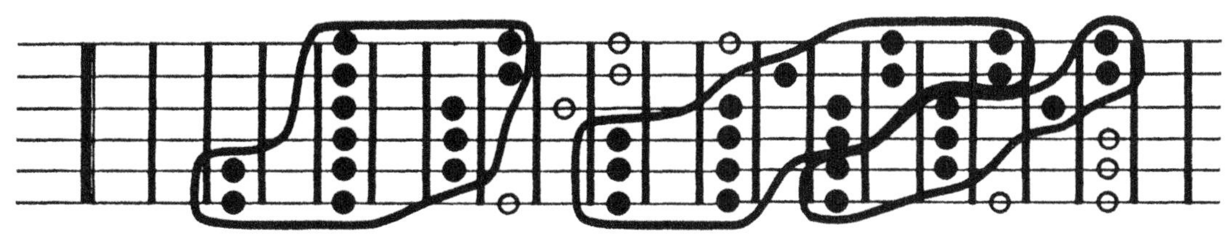

Major Pentatonic Scales

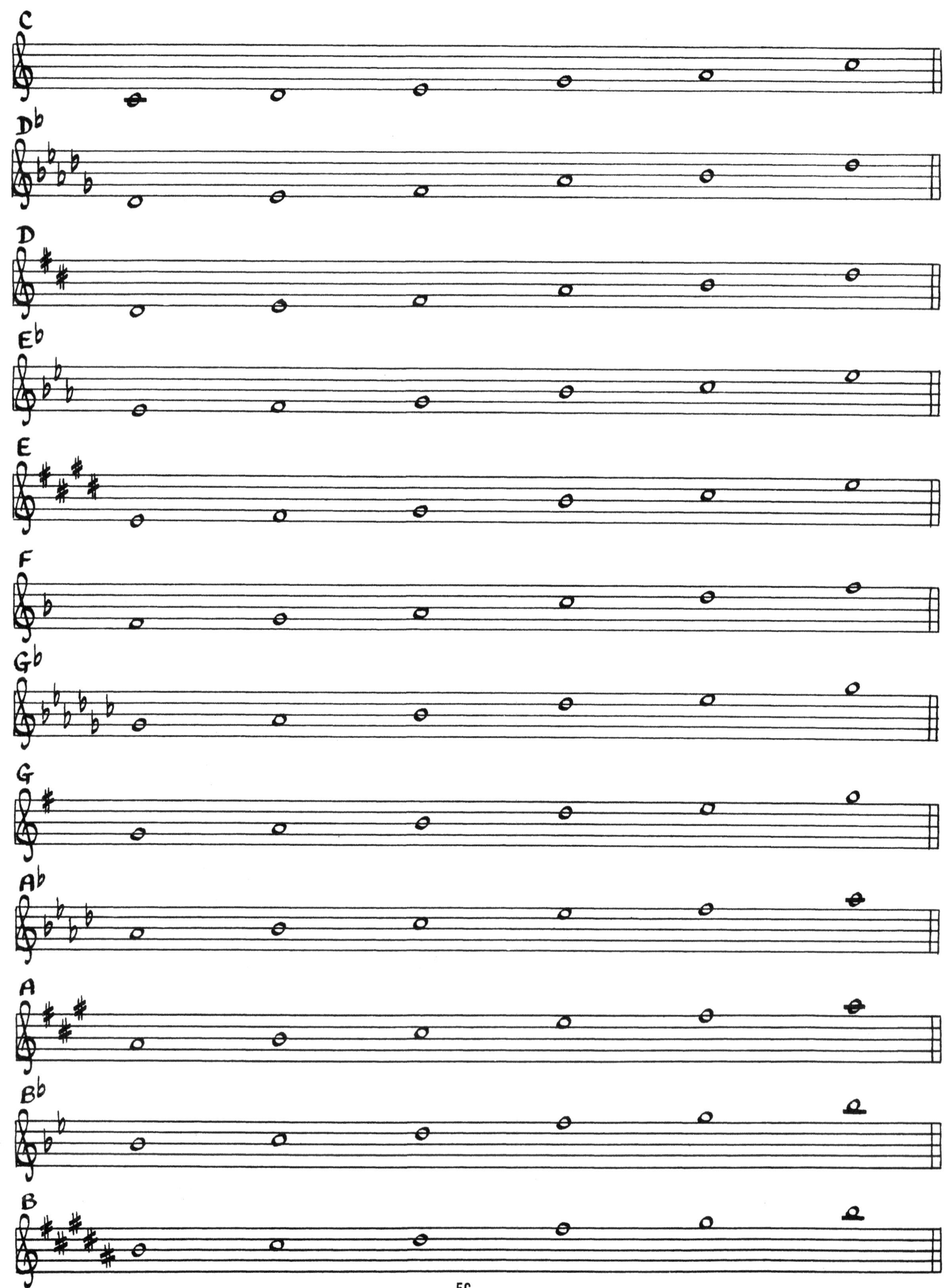

Pentatonics over major 7th chords

We can play the Pentatonic scales based on the 1st, 2nd and 5th degrees of a major 7th, to give us good inside sounding material. So using Cmaj7 chord as our example we could play the pentatonic scales below:

□ Key Note

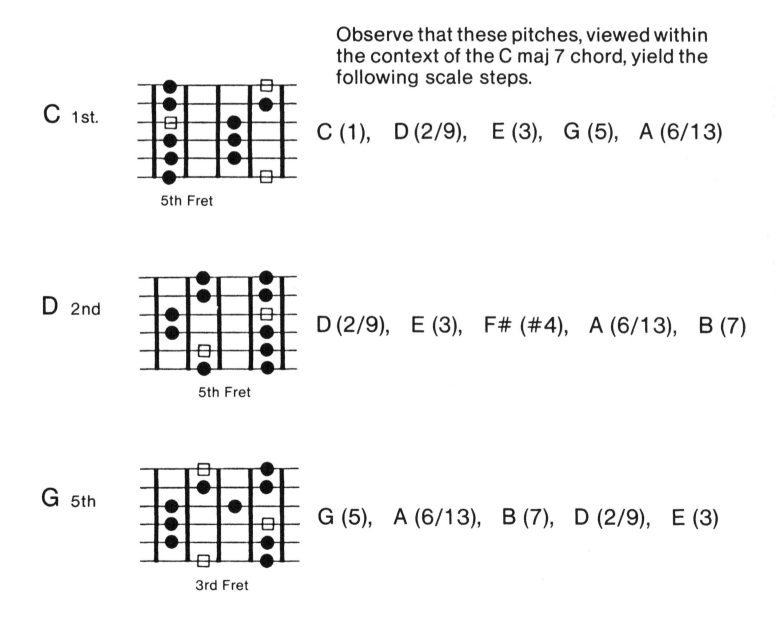

Observe that these pitches, viewed within the context of the C maj 7 chord, yield the following scale steps.

C 1st.

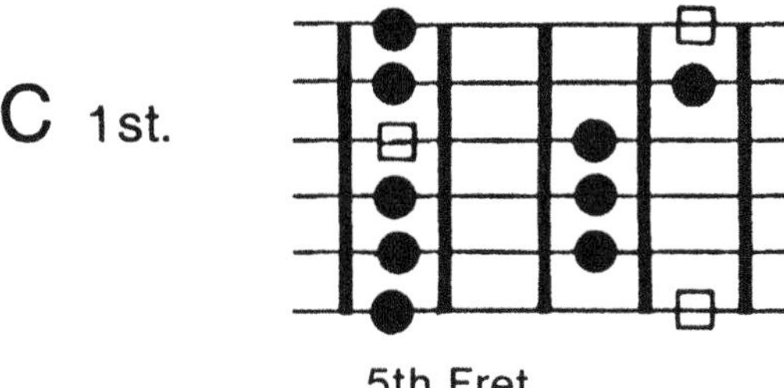

5th Fret

C (1), D (2/9), E (3), G (5), A (6/13)

D 2nd

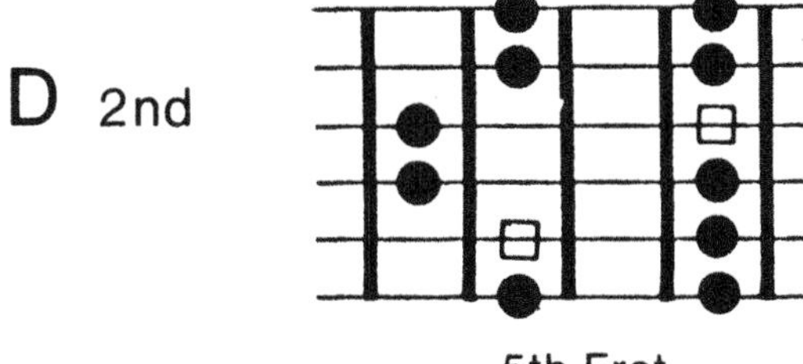

5th Fret

D (2/9), E (3), F# (#4), A (6/13), B (7)

G 5th

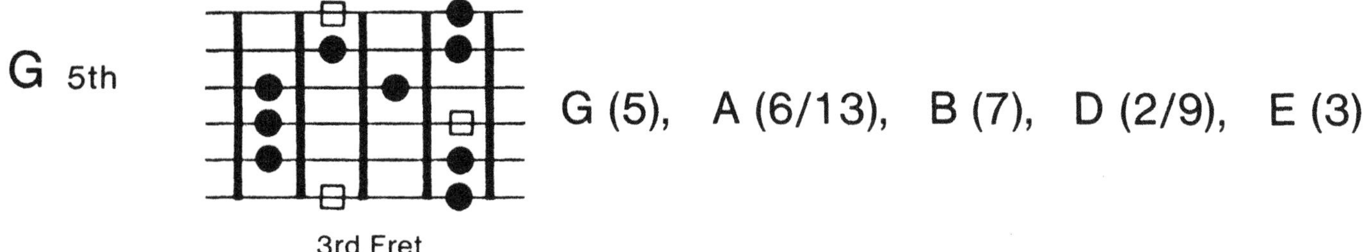

3rd Fret

G (5), A (6/13), B (7), D (2/9), E (3)

Pentatonic over the Minor 7th chord

We can play the Pentatonic scale based on the Minor 3rd, Perfect 4th and Minor 7th tones over the root of a Minor 7th chord to give us good inside sounding material. Using Cminor7 chord as our example we could play the Pentatonic scales below:

□ Key Note

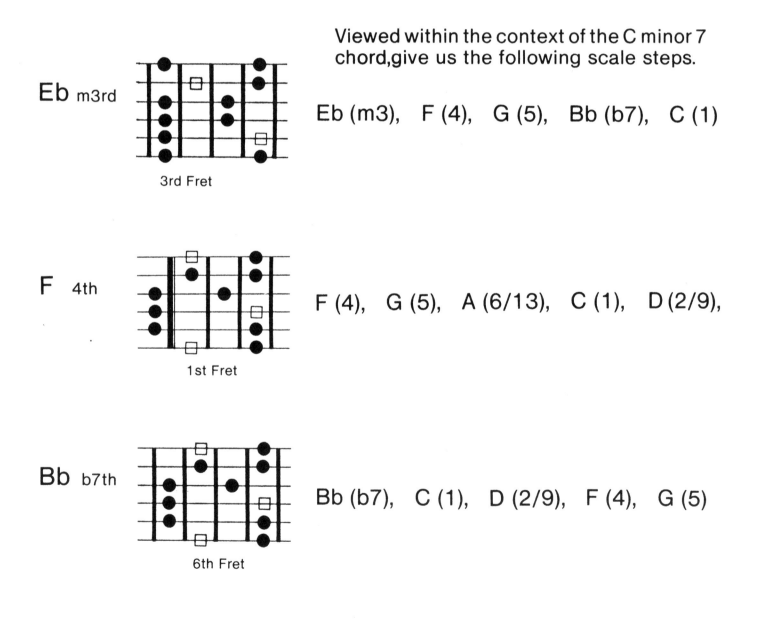

Viewed within the context of the C minor 7 chord,give us the following scale steps.

Eb m3rd

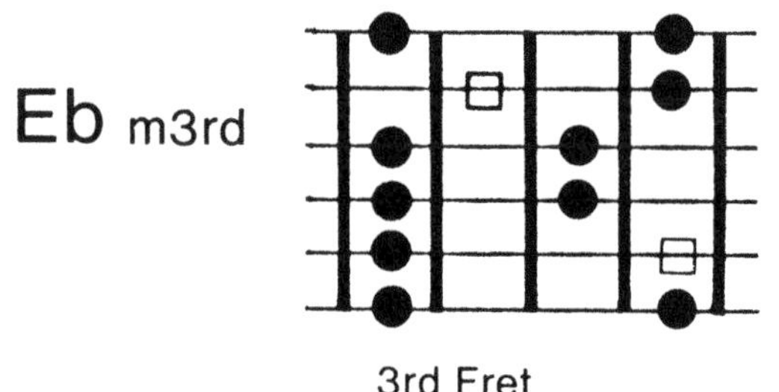

3rd Fret

Eb (m3), F (4), G (5), Bb (b7), C (1)

F 4th

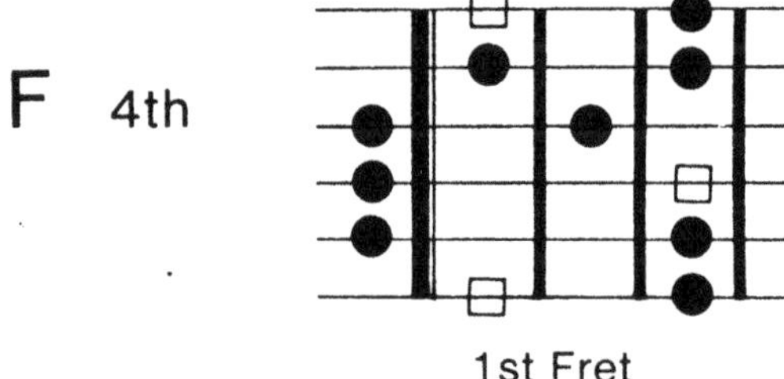

1st Fret

F (4), G (5), A (6/13), C (1), D (2/9),

Bb b7th

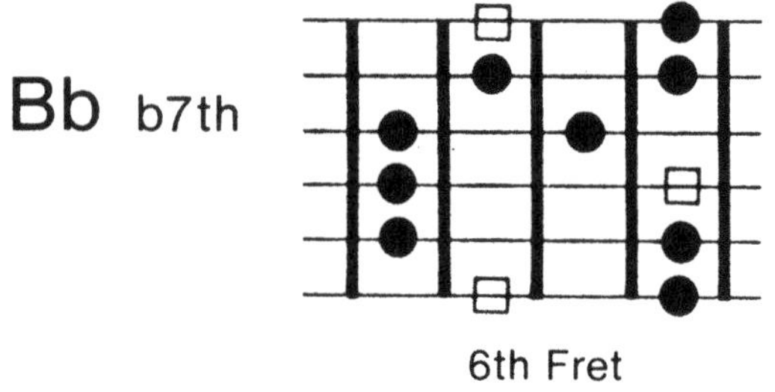

6th Fret

Bb (b7), C (1), D (2/9), F (4), G (5)

In the example below use the correct Pentatonic scales for the Minor 7th chords and as we've discussed on the previous page the correct Pentatonic scales over the Major 7th chords.

Sometimes the mind gets bored and fatiqued by the repetitiousness of practicing. Be creative, pick out the notes you like and play those. Make up patterns, play in short burst, no more than 10 to 20 minutes at a time, but several times a day.

Pentatonic over the Dominant 7th chord

We can play the pentatonic scales based on the Root (or tonic), minor 3rd, and dom. 7th degrees of the dominant 7th chord. With C7 chord as our example we could play the following pentatonic scales.

□ Key Note

Viewed within the context of the C dom. 7 chord give us the following scale steps.

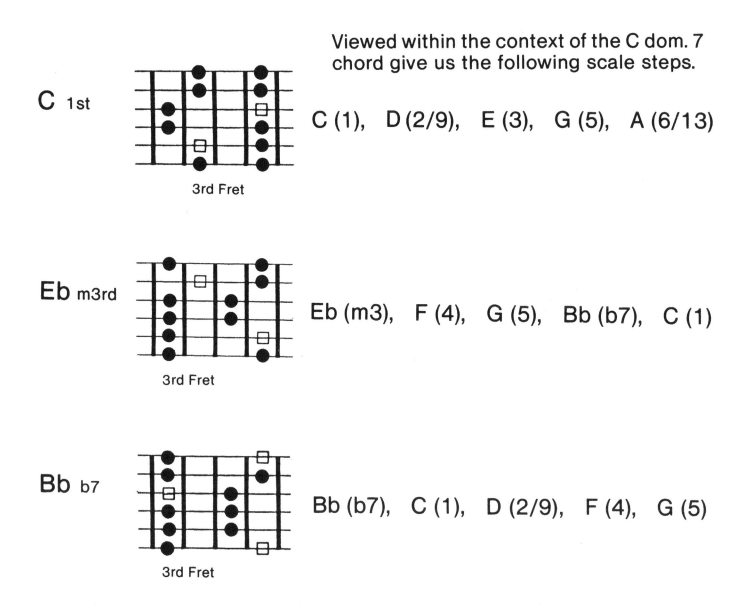

C 1st

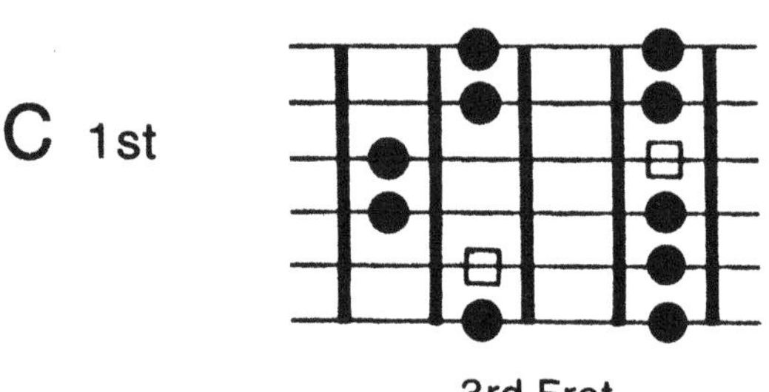

3rd Fret

C (1), D (2/9), E (3), G (5), A (6/13)

Eb m3rd

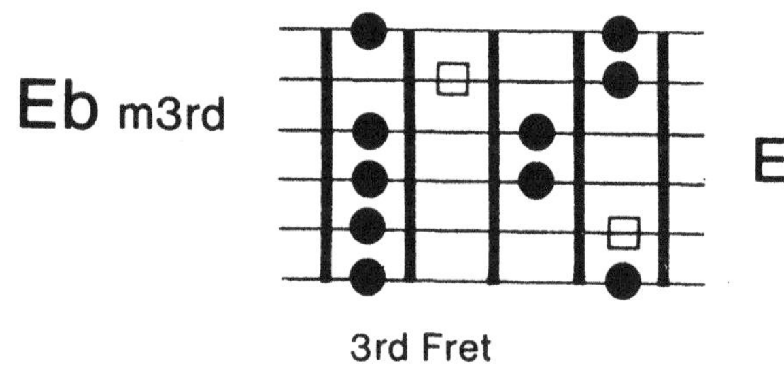

3rd Fret

Eb (m3), F (4), G (5), Bb (b7), C (1)

Bb b7

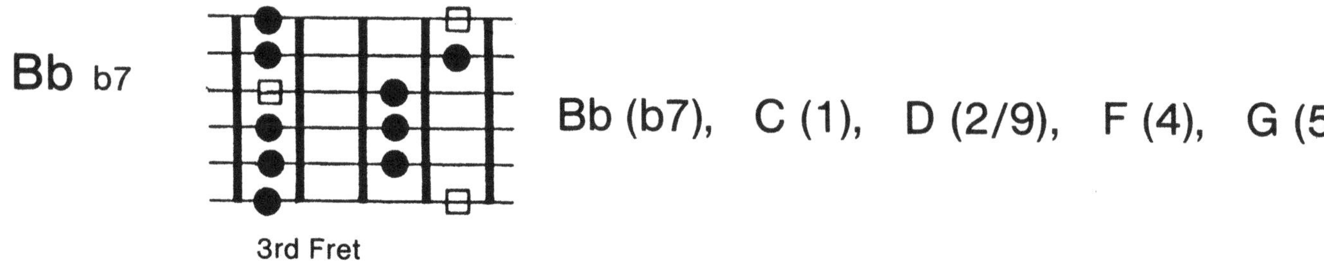

Bb (b7), C (1), D (2/9), F (4), G (5)

3rd Fret

Now turn yourself loose with all your pentatonic skills as you improvise against these changes.

Em7 | Am7 | D7 | G Maj.7

C Maj.7 | G7 | B Maj.7 |

Bm7 | Em7 | A7 | D Maj.7

G Maj.7 | D♭7 | G♭ |

D♭7 | | G♭ |

B♭7 | | E♭ | B7

Em7 | Am7 | D7 | G Maj.7

C Maj.7 | C mi | G Maj.7 | B♭°

Am7 | D7 | G | B7

Connecting Pentatonic scales over Chord Changes

These and of course all the other scales should be practiced so that you could move instantly over chord changes from any one point in the scale to another, without running through the scale steps consecutively.

If we take the ever popular II7, V7, I7 change and look at the pentatonic possibilities given for each chord in the key of C we'd have the following;

Function	**II7**	**V7**	**I7**
Name	**Dm7**	**G7**	**Cmaj.7**
Pentatonic	**F, G, C**	**G, Bb, F**	**C, D, G**

NOW LETS CONSIDER THESE POSSIBILTIES:
1. Notice the G pentatonic works over all three chords. We could stay in one scale over all three chord changes or...
2. C Pentatonic could be moved conveniently to Bb in the II7-V7 change, just move back two frets. But now maybe you want to change from Bb to F pentatonic over the G7 chord. What to do? Well two possable things,one, just slide down five frets, By moving back five frets would enable us to duplacate the SAME PATTERN, the fingering would be the same just at a different pitch. Or we could stay in the same position and just ALTER THE FORM. Thereby keeping in the same pitch range.

Have a friend play the II7, V7, I7 changes as you play the two patterns below.

Bb Pentatonic

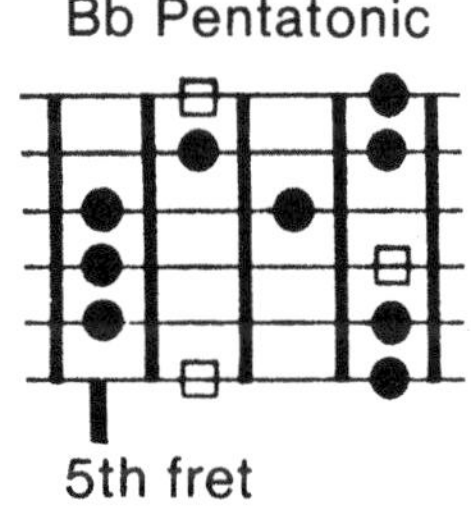

F Pentatonic

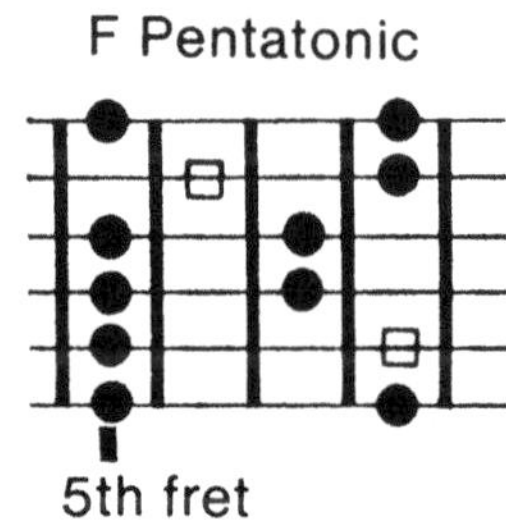

Minor Pentatonics

New application of an old scale

The minor pentatonics aren't really new scales, not new to your fingers at least. If you've been studing the last several pages you'r fingers already know all the pentatonic forms there is, for the minor pentatonics we need only change the way in which we VIEW THE SCALE, thus we only CHANGE THE ROOT OR TONIC.

Now lets look at the relationship between the major and minor pentatonics.

Major pentatonic built on the 1st, 2nd, 3rd, 5th, and 6th of the major diatonic scale.

Key of C

Minor pentatonic built on the 1st, b3rd, 4th, 5th, and b7th.

A Minor Pentatonic

Below are the fingering patterns for the major and minor pentatonics, as you can see it's the ROOT NOTE THAT IS DIFFERENT

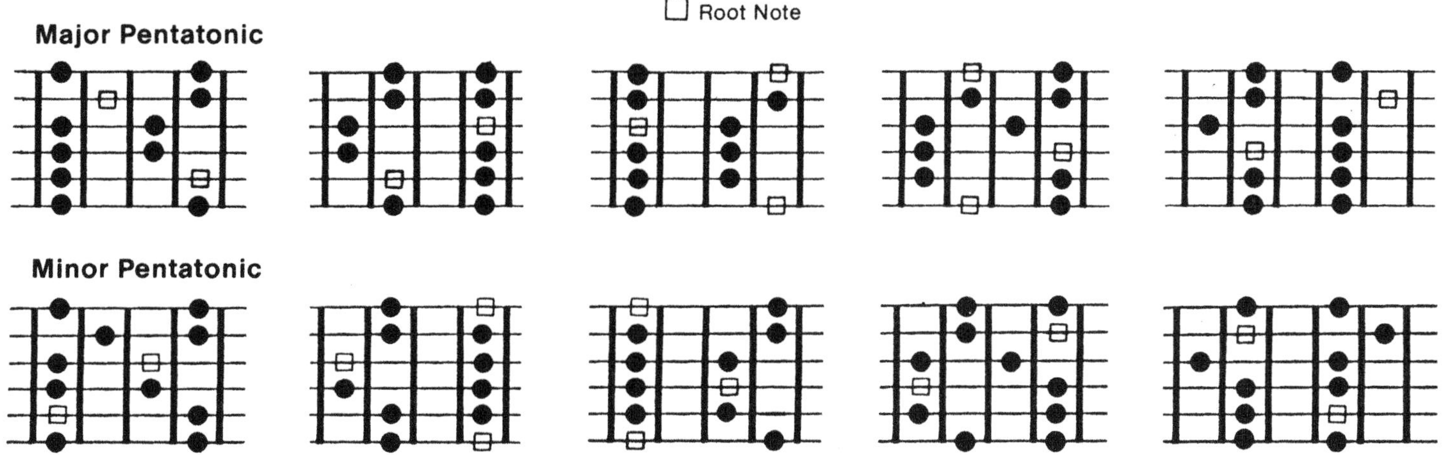

Minor Pentatonic Scales

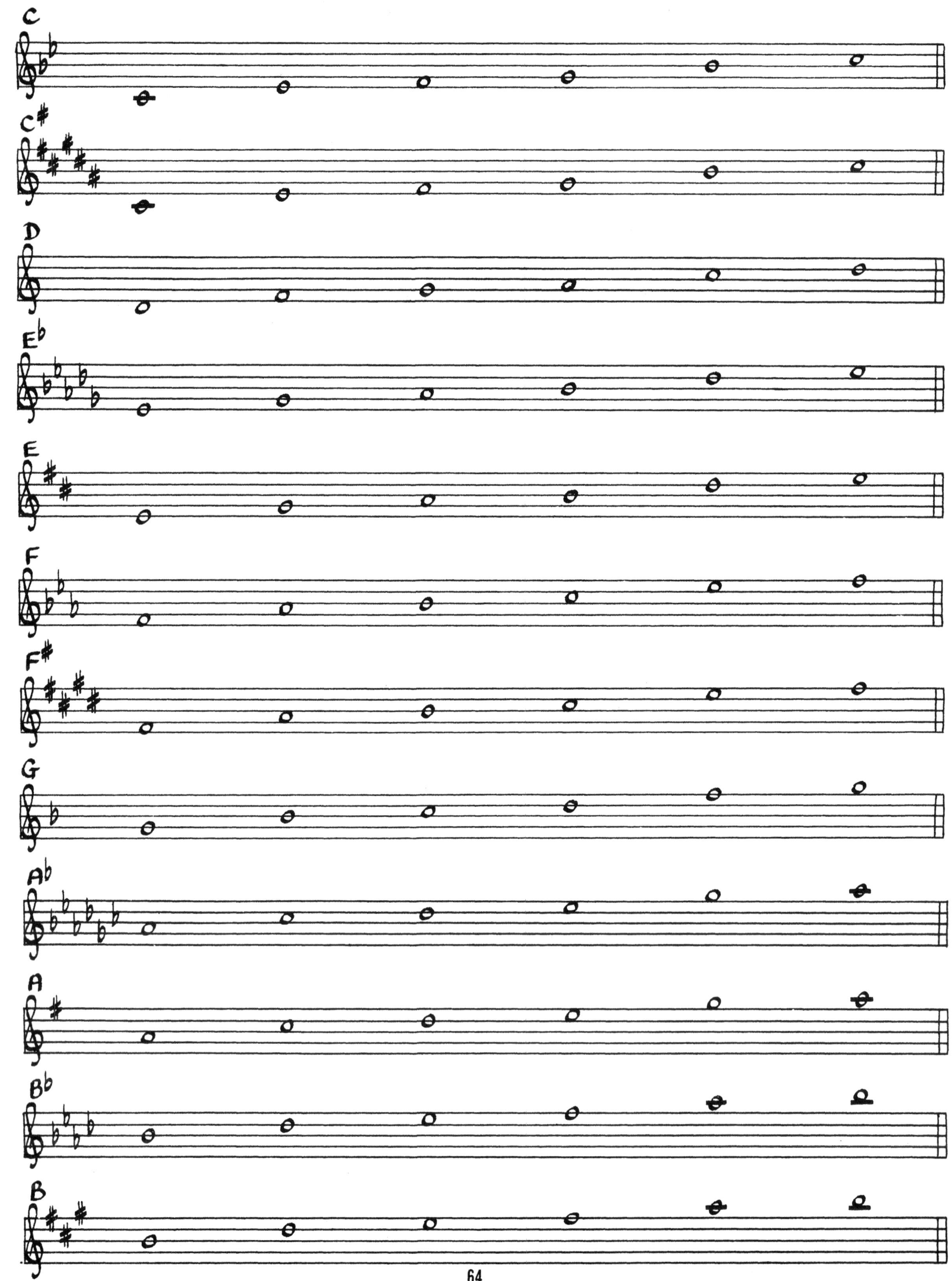

Application of Minor Pentatonic

The Minor Pentatonic scale may be used over minor harmony.

Play you're own line over the following progressions.

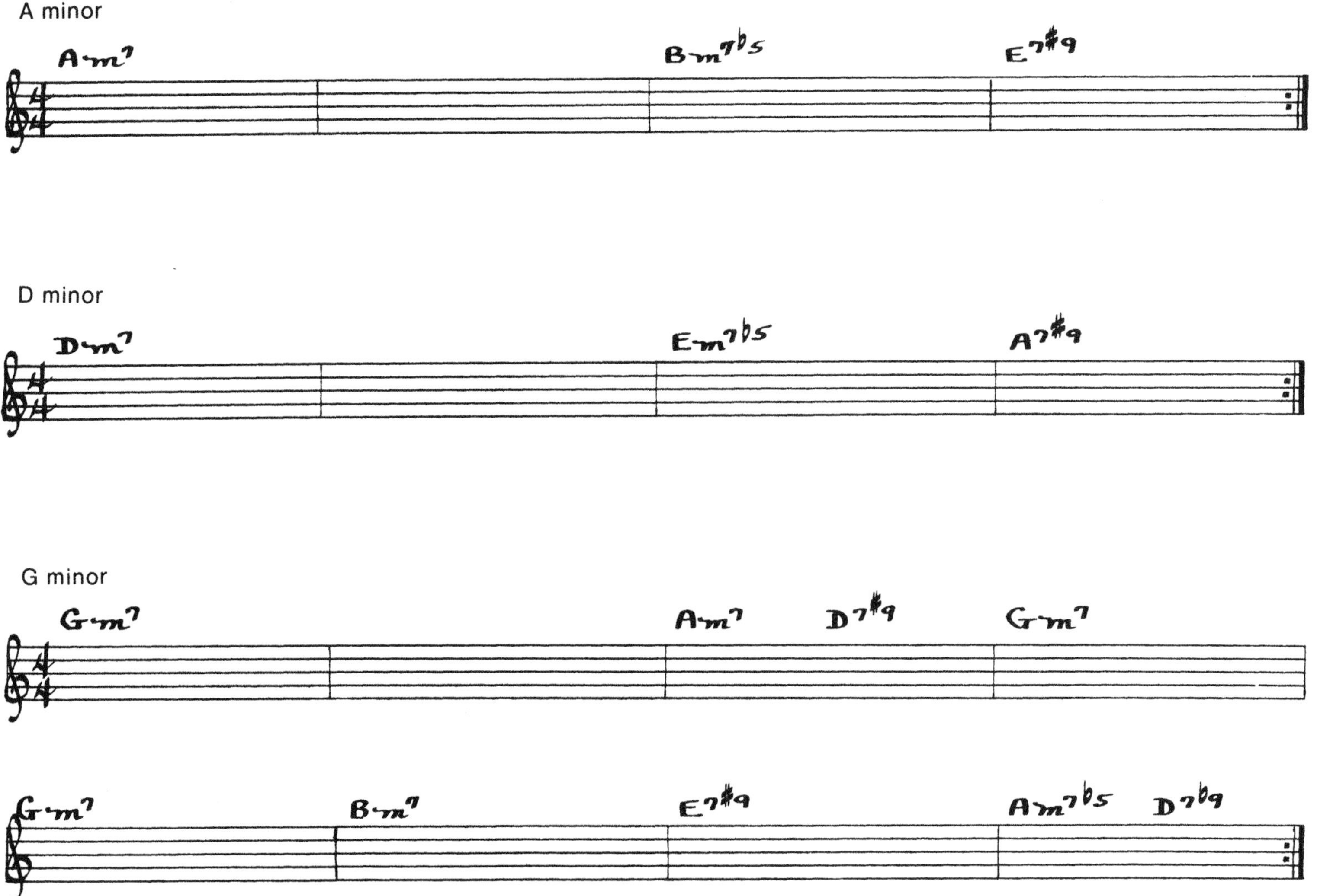

Have someone play the chord changes or tape them yourself and find the right pentatonic that sounds good to you. Watch out for that whole-tone scale at the first ending.

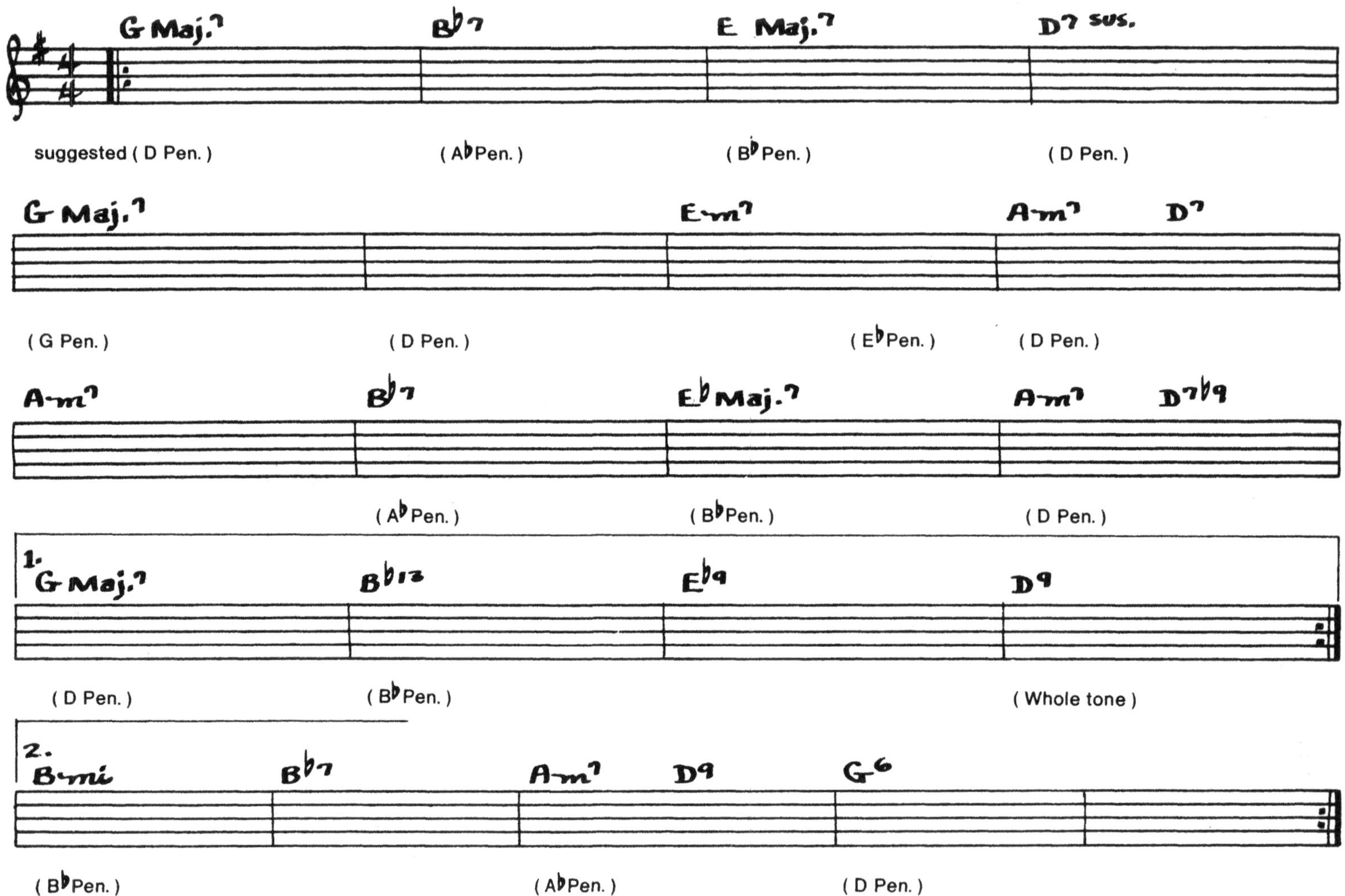

Scales transforming obstacles into tools

Altered Pentatonics

Try altering any tone of the pentatonic scale and it's modes by a ½ step and apply it to various chords.

Let's say you play a D pentatonic over a C7 chord. All the notes will sound good except one and thats the B natural, if you want to play "outside" it's alright to play the D Pentatonic with NO alternations. However, if you want to play "inside" and make all the notes in the scale compatable with the chord tones, you'll have to ALTER the B natural by lowering it one half step to Bb.

Altered Pentatonics Over Dominant Chords

Construct a pentatonic with a lowered 5th note on the 2nd and b6 scale steps, or a pentatonic with a lowered 2nd note on the ROOT, b3rd, b5th, or 6th.

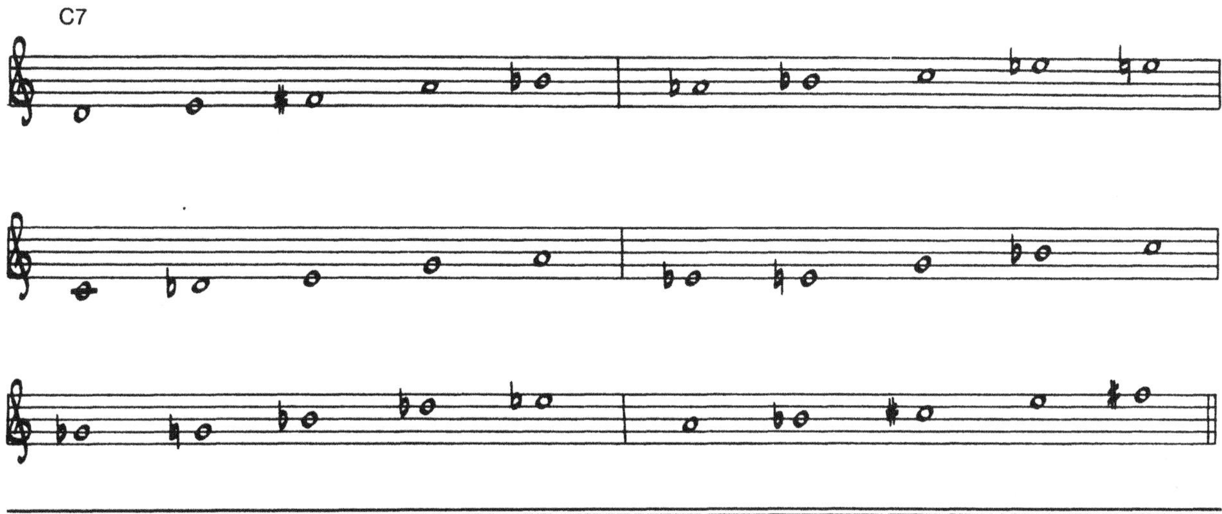

Altered Pentatonics Over Diminished 7th Chords

Since all the notes in every unaltered pentatonic scale will clash with a Diminished 7th chord, try this, construct an altered pentatonic scale ONE STEP ABOVE any note in the chord and LOWER THE 2nd SCALE STEP.

Using the C Major Pentatonic scale as our example, let's veiw it within the contents of various chords.

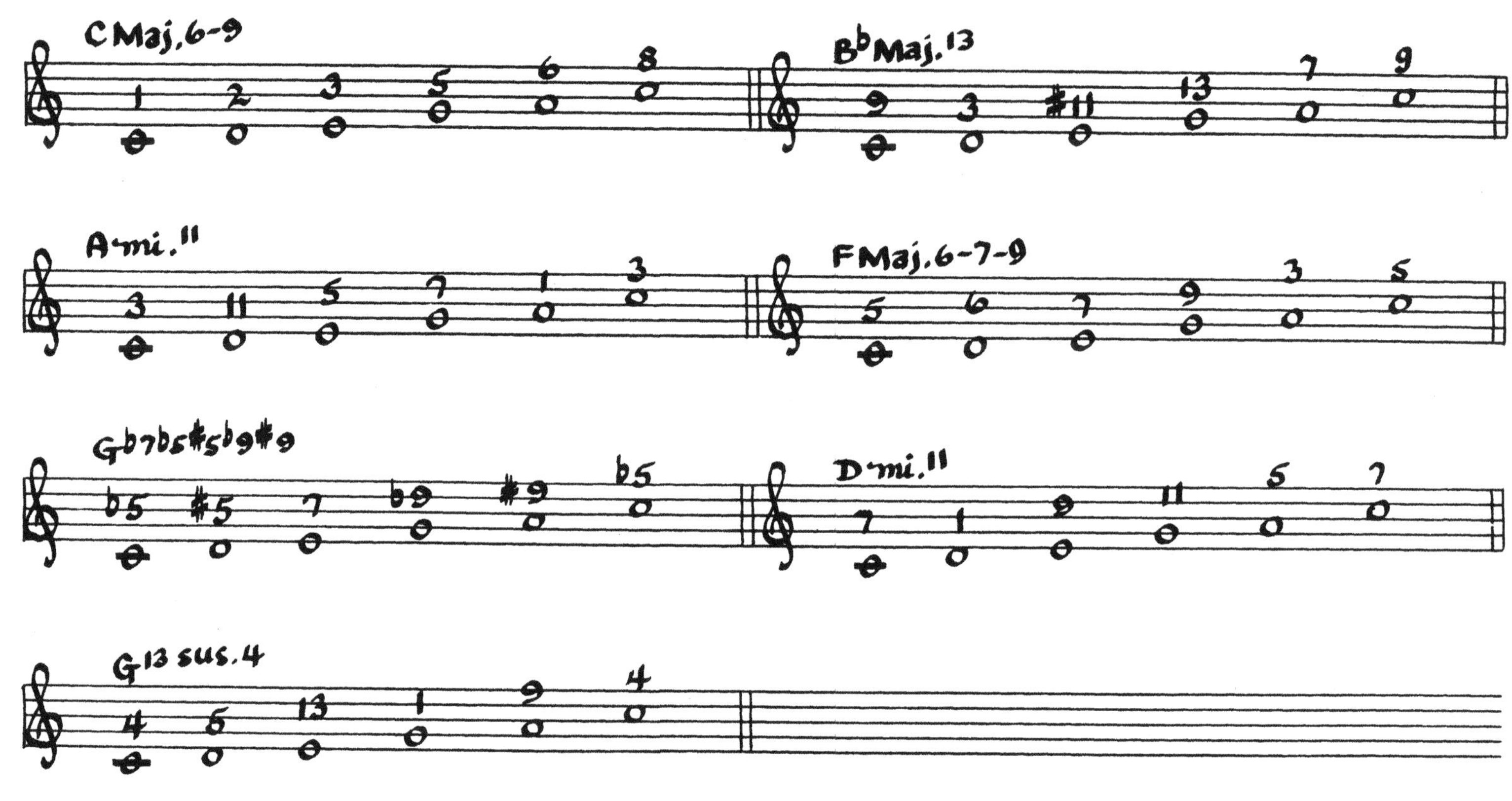

Using the C Minor Pentatonic scale as our example, let's veiw it within the contents of various chords.

Summary

No Rules...Just Some Basic Concepts

For Country or Rock the minor pentatonic built on the 6th scale step will sound best against major chords. Example:

C major------use A minor pentatonic
G major------use E minor pentatonic
E major------use C# minor pentatonic
A major------use F# minor pentatonic

To create a more "outside" sound, try a pentatonic scale from a root a half step above or below the root of the chord you're playing against.

Try playing pentatonics on each chromatic tone.

Try altering any tone of the pentatonic scale and it's modes by a 1/2 step and apply it to various chord types.

For major 7th chords play pentatonics built on the 1st, 2nd, and 5th steps of the major scale.

For minor 7th chords play pentatonics built on the b3rd, b7th and 4th of the major scale.

For minor 7th-5 chords play pentatonics built on the b5, b6,and b2.

For dominant 7th chords play pentatonics built on the 1st, b3rd, b5th b7th,steps and the 4th for the suspended 4th chords.

Diminished chords--use altered pentatonics, construct a pentatonic scale ONE STEP ABOVE any note in the diminished 7th chord, then lower the 2nd note in the scale.

Playing a pentatonic scale a minor third above the tonic of a major, we automatically produce two distinctively BLUESY notes, the flatted 3rd, and the flatted 7th.

Don't use pentatonics exclusively, mix them with other harmonic material.

Use pentatonics in sequences.

"The knowledge of the particular structure (the location of half-steps within the scale) is essential to the accomplished improviser." Scales often need to be constructed SPONTANEOUSLY within an improvised solo, understanding of the scale structure will allow this.

Harmonic Minor Scale

The Harmonic Minor Scale is constructed of 3 whole steps, 3 half steps and an augmented 2nd (minor 3rd). The half steps occur between steps 2 and 3, steps 5 and 6, and steps 7 and 8. The augmented 2nd occurs between steps 6 and 7.

Key note □

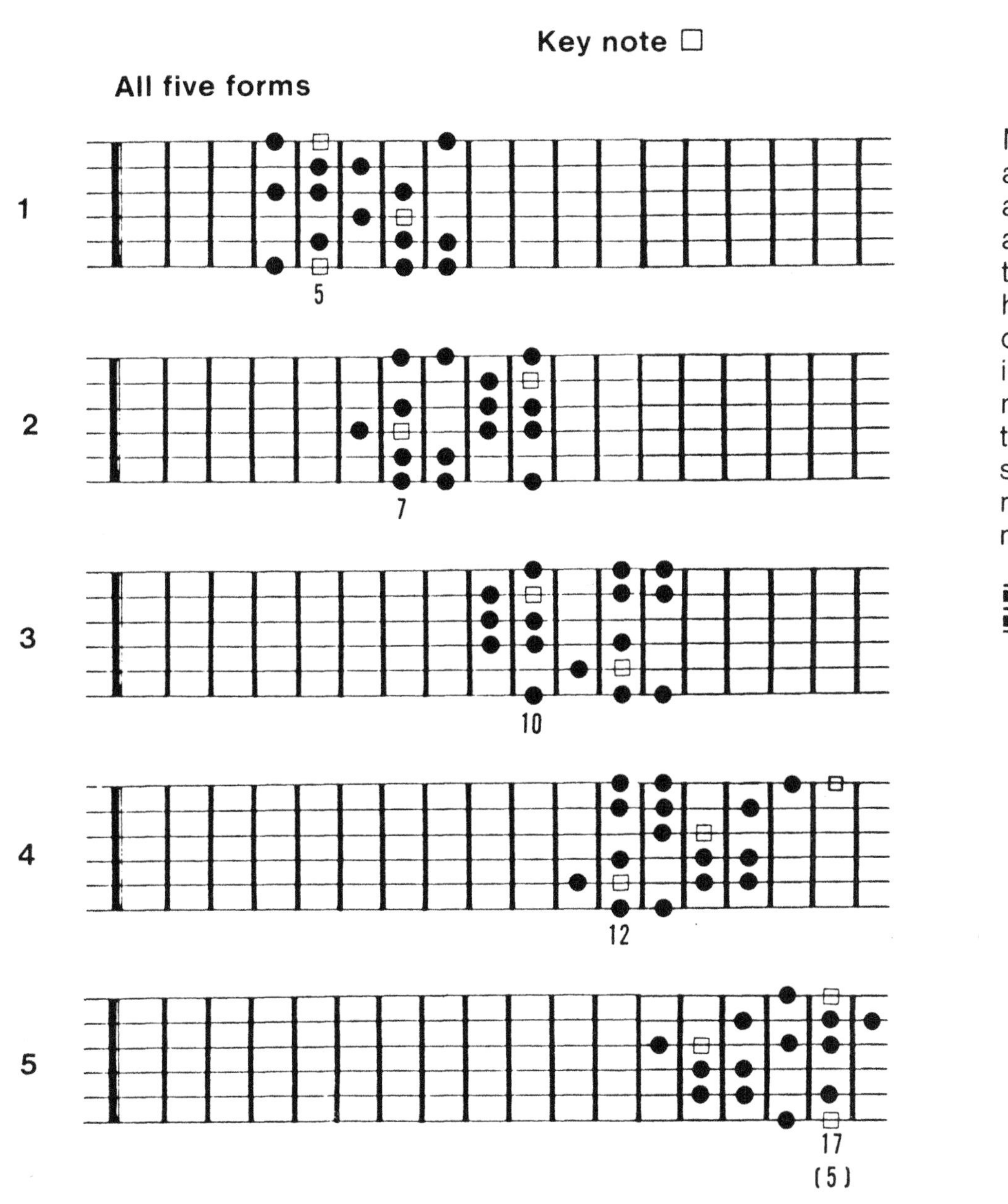

Notice in the above example that the harmonic and natural minor scales are the same, except that the seventh step in the harmonic minor is raised one half step. It's this interval skip of an augmented second (or minor third) that makes this scale different from the natural (relative) and melodic minor scale.

Harmonic Minor Scales

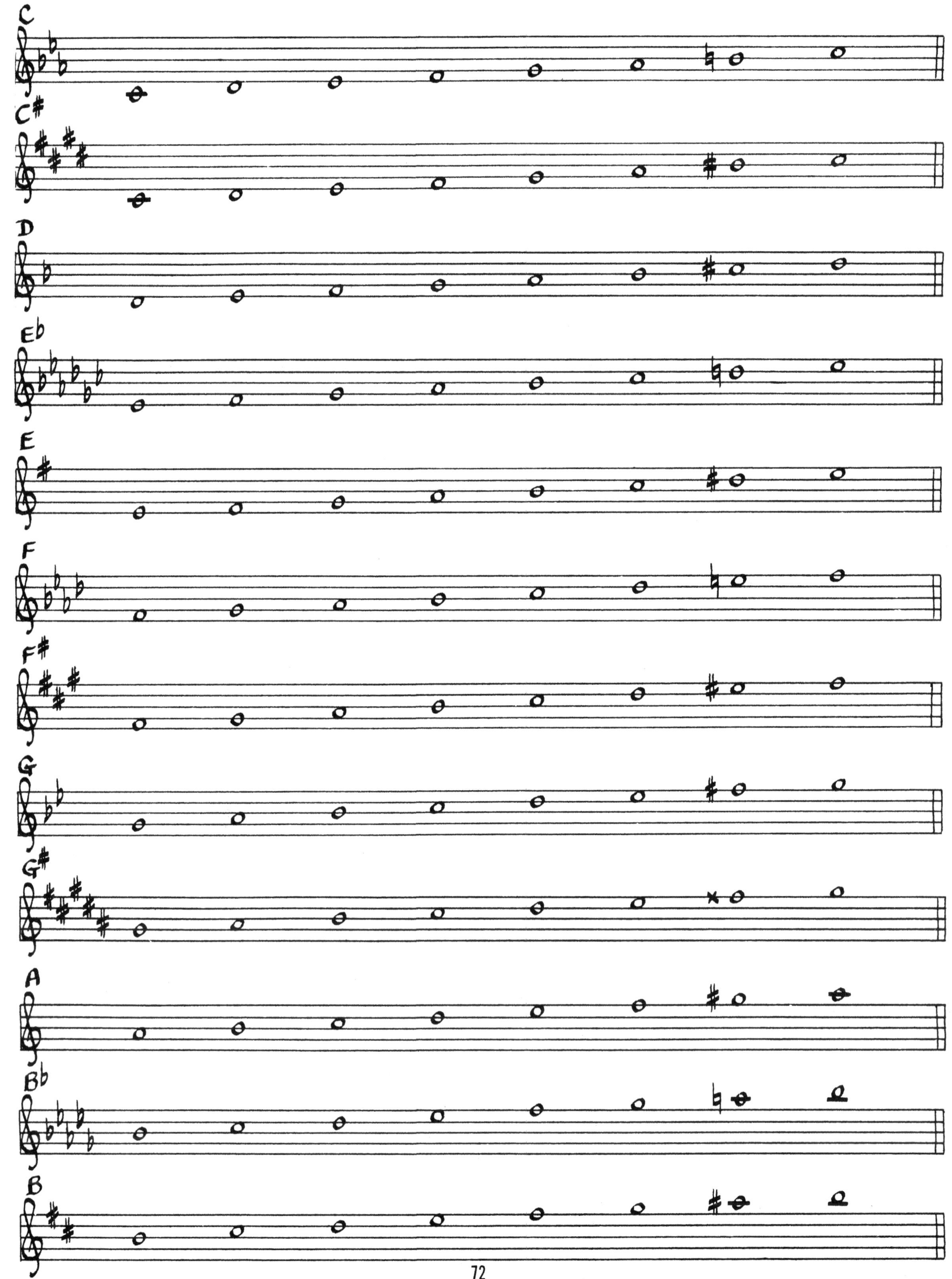

First Application

In its simplest role, it fits a minor chord WITH A MAJOR 7th called Minor-Major 7th the usual progression is where a voice starts on the Tonic note of the chord and moves down by half steps, ending on the 6th. See the example below:

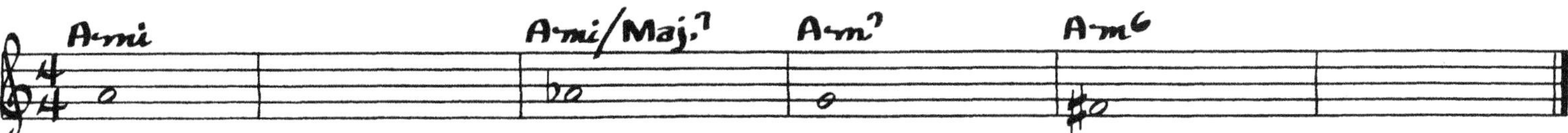

In the above exercise use the natural minor scale for all chords except the Am/Maj 7 then use the Harmonic Minor Scale.

Second Application

The "A" Harmonic Minor Scale is also good against the E7 chord and adds some alterations along the way. Let's see why! If we begin the same scale on E going from E to E and looked at within the context of the E chord, we have the following scale steps:

E	F	G#	A	B	C	D	E
1	b9	3	4	5	#5(b13)	b7	8

All the notes of the E7 chord are there; the E, G#, B, and D along with the b9 and b13, so we have a new rule for this application:

Rule: If you have a Dominant Chord with a b9 or b13 (or#5) go up a perfect fourth from the root of the chord and play that harmonic minor scale.

Example:
1. A7#5b9--use D harmonic minor scale.
2. Bb7b9b13--Eb harmonic minor scale.
3. G7b9b13--?
4. C7b9b13--?
5. F7b9b13--?

Third Application

Use "A" Harmonic Minor Scale over D7

Let's rewrite the scale beginning on D

D	E	F	G#	A	B	C	D
1	9	#9	#4b5	5	13(6)	b7	8
		(b3#11)					

As you'll notice most of the notes of the D7 chord are there ie: D, A, and C the 3rd is absent. But may be added to the scale, especially in the lower registers, where it will not clash with the #9 (the enharmonic equivalent of the minor 3rd).

General Rule: For a Dominant Chord with a #9 and a #11 go up a fifth from the root of the chord, and play that harmonic minor and add the major 3rd if needed.

Example:

1. F7#9 or #11--play C harmonic minor scale starting on F
2. C7#11--play G harmonic minor scale starting on C
3. D7#11--?
4. G7b9--?
5. Eb7#b5--?

We have to know

where any given scale may be used.

Modes Generated by the Harmonic Minor Scale

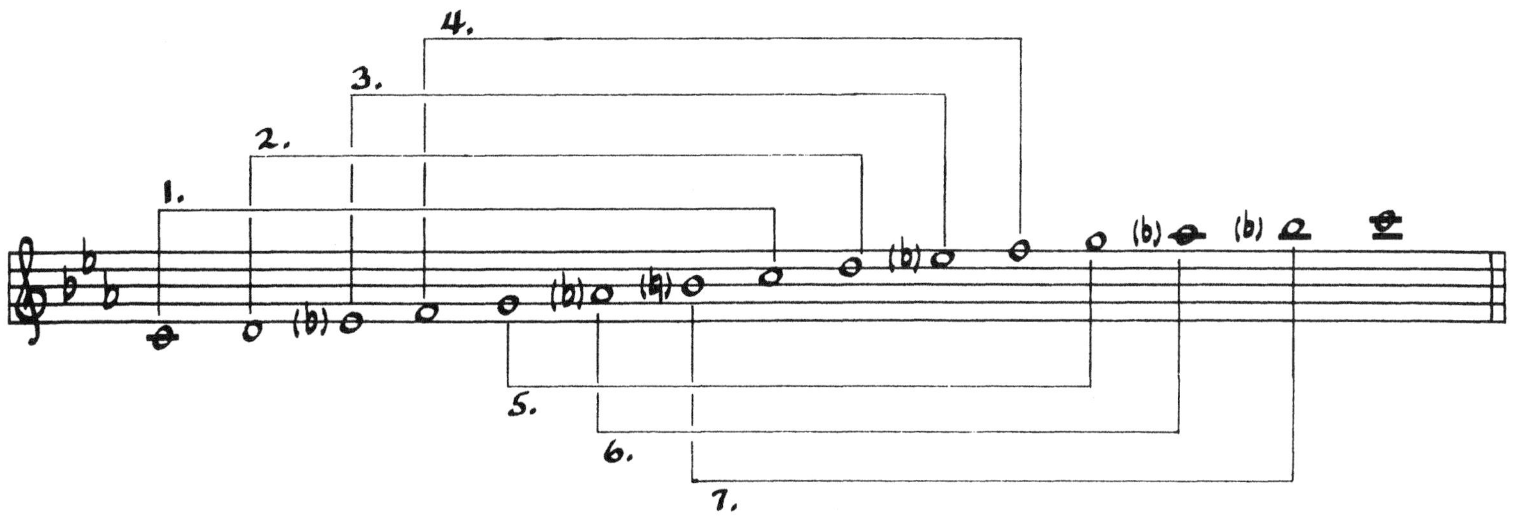

Application

1. C to C, used with Cmi#7 chord.
2. D to D, used with Dmi7-5 chord.
3. Ebto Eb, used with Eb maj7#5 chord.
4. F to F, used with Fmi7 chord.
5. G to G, used with G7-9 chord.
6. Ab to Ab, used with Abmaj.7 chord.
7. B to B, used with B dim7.

The Harmonic Minor is used mostly with the I, II, and V, chords (this is expecially true at a II, V, I, cadence point in a minor key). The other modes tend to function as synthetic scale forms that might be substituted for a more conventional scale. Only the first mode is included here. Remember mode 3 could be used with a Major 7#5. Mode 4 with a Mi7. etc.

Melodic Minor Scales

The Ascending Melodic Minor Scale

A altered Natural (pure) minor scale, the ascending melodic minor scale is constructed of 5 whole steps and 2 hald steps. The half steps occur between steps 2 and 3 and steps 7 and 8 of the scale.

C Melodic Minor

Two ways of conceiving a Melodic Minor Scale:

1. A Pure Minor Scale with a raised 6th and 7th scale steps.

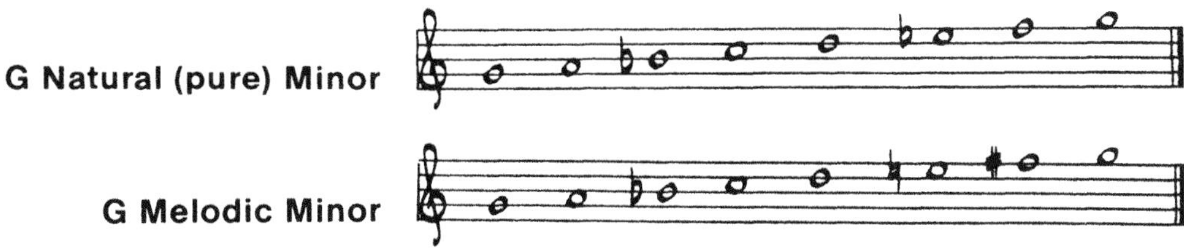

2. A Major scale with a lowered 3rd.

Application

This scale is used with minor family chords that have a raised 7th. It can also be implied by playing the raised 7th scale step as a passing tone between the root and 7th of a regular minor 7th chord.

When the scale is used with a minor#7 chord, example Cm #7, or Cm/maj7, any scale tone can be emphasized or leaned on. All are considered strong notes. With one exception the root of the chord has a tendency to resolve downward to the raised 7th of the chord.

Combined Melodic Minor Scales

In it's conventional form the scale is shown DESCENDING in the natural minor form.

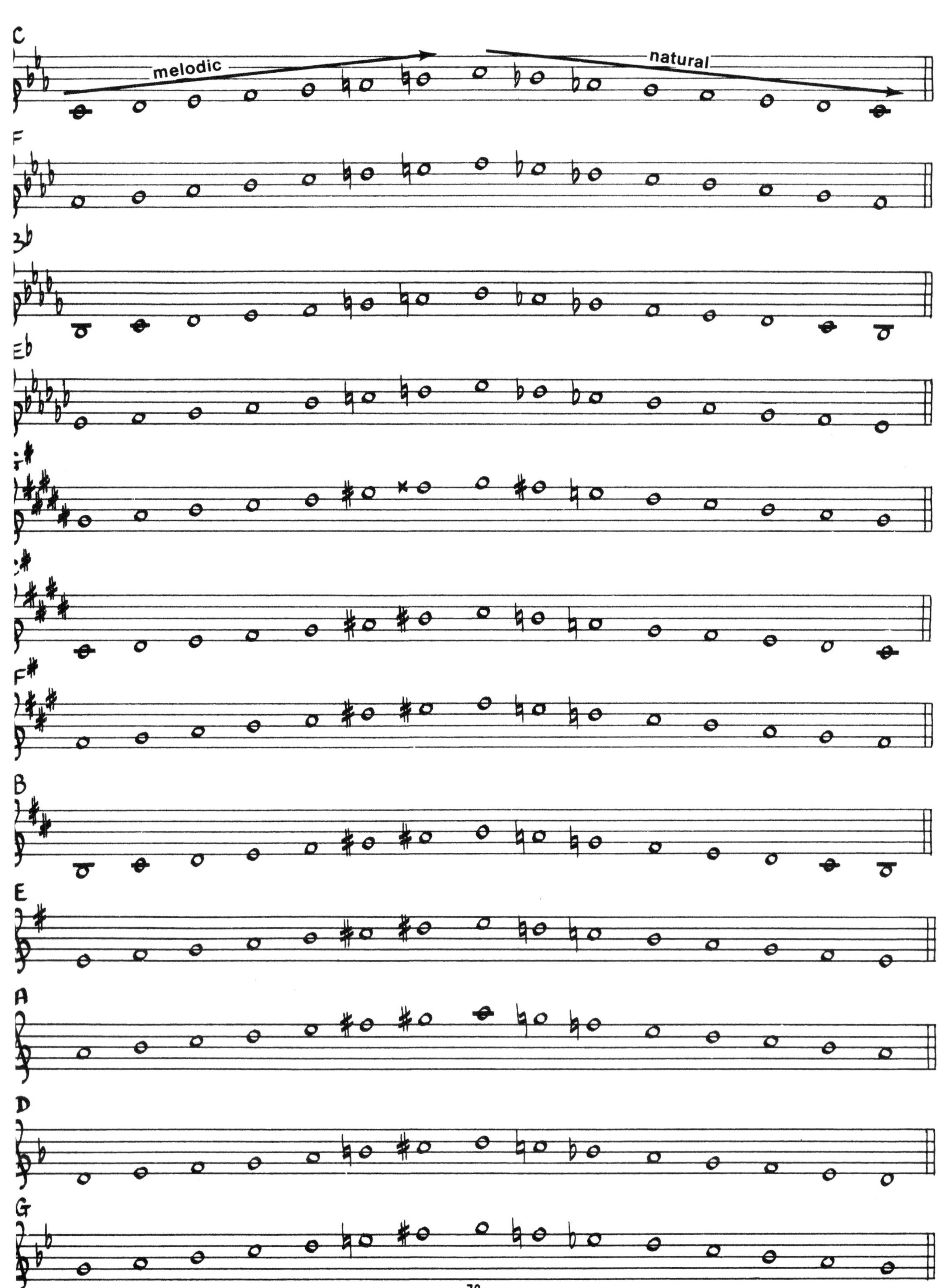

Modes Generated By The Ascending Melodic Minor Scale

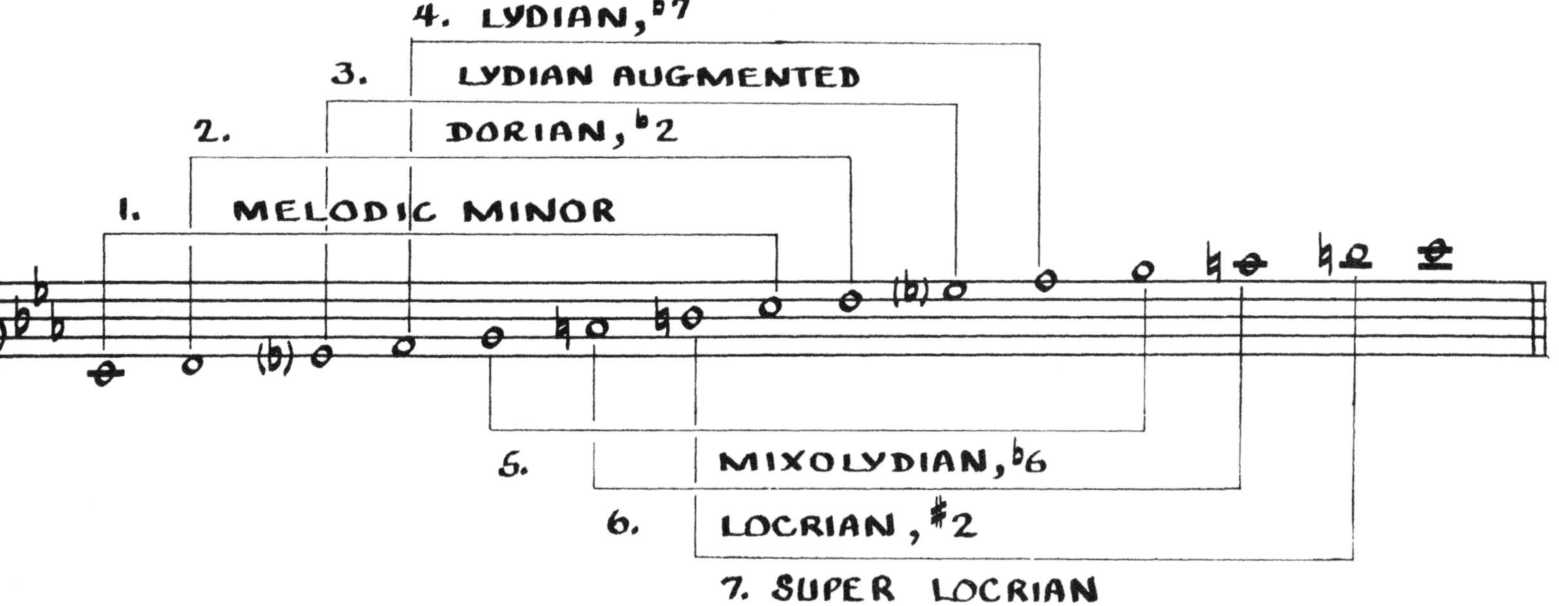

Based on C Melodic Minor Scale

1. C to C, The C Melodic Minor Scale
2. D to D, The D Dorian, b2 Scale (uncommon)
3. Eb to Eb, The Eb Lydian Augmented Scale
4. F to F. The F Lydian, b7 Scale
5. G to G, The Mixolydian, b6 Scale (uncommon)
6. A to A, The Locrian, #2 Scale
7. B to B, The Super Locrian Scale

Lydian-Augmented Scale

This scale is constructed of 5 whole steps and 2 half steps, the half steps are between steps 5 and 6, and steps 7 and 8 of the scale.

C Lydian Augmented

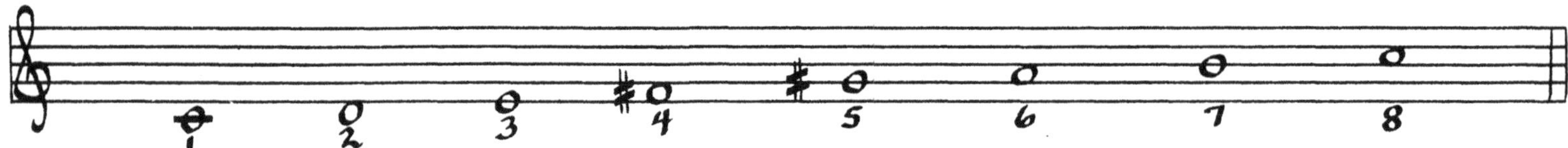

FINGERING

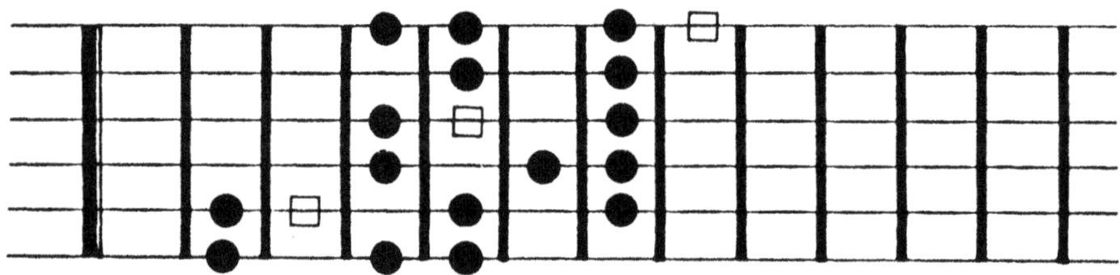

Two ways of conceiving a Lydian-Augmented scale.

1. A major scale with a raised 4th and 5th scale step.

2. A scale having the same tones as a melodic minor scale built on the note three half steps below. (C Lydian-Augmented is the same as A melodic minor).

Application

The Lydian-Augmented scale is used with a major family chord which has a raised 5th. The #11 altho in the scale does not have to be present in the harmony.

As in the major scale, the root note may sound off to the major 7th of the chord. And should resolve downward to the 7th. All other notes can be emphasized.

Lydian Augmented Scales

Lydian, b7 Scale

This Lydian,b7 scale is often called the Lydian-Dominant. It is constructed of 5 whole steps and 2 half steps. The half steps occur between steps 4 and 5 and steps 6 and 7.

C Lydian,♭7

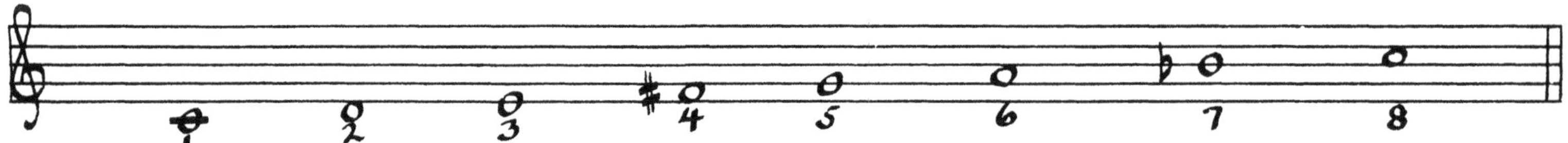

FINGERING

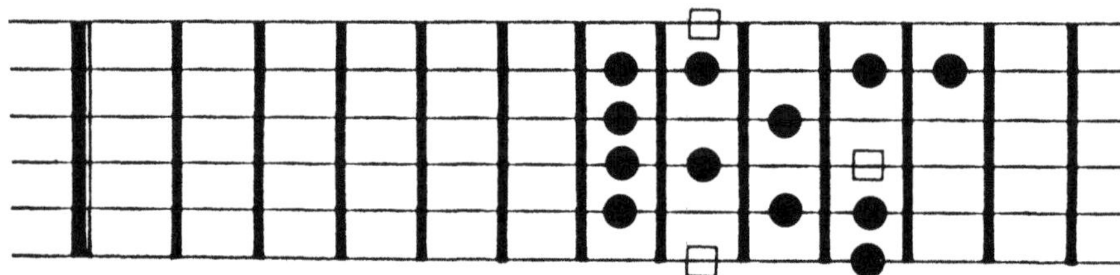

Three ways of conceiving a Lydian,b7 scale:

1. A Lydian scale with a lowered 7th scale step.
2. A scale having the same tones as a melocic minor scale built on the note a perfect 4th below. (C Lydian,b7 is the same as G Melodic minor).
3. A Mixolydian scale with a raised 4th scale step.

Application

Used with dominant family chords that is unaltered with the exception of the #11 that may or may not be present. The dissonance (or wrong sounding) note of the unaltered 4th disappears by raising the 4th of the mixolydian mode in createing this scale and any tone of the scale maybe emphasized.

When the #11 is in a dominant chord the lydian, b7 scale might be a better choice over the mixolydian scale. Because the unaltered 4th of the mixolydian mode would cause a clash with the #11.

A Lydian, b7 scale has the same tones as the Super Locrian scale built on the note located a tri-tone above or below.

Lydian, ♭7 Scales

Locrian, #2 Scale

The Locrian,#2 scale is constructed of 5 whole steps and 2 half steps. The half steps occuring between steps 2 and 3 and steps 4 and 5 of the scale.

C Locrian♮2

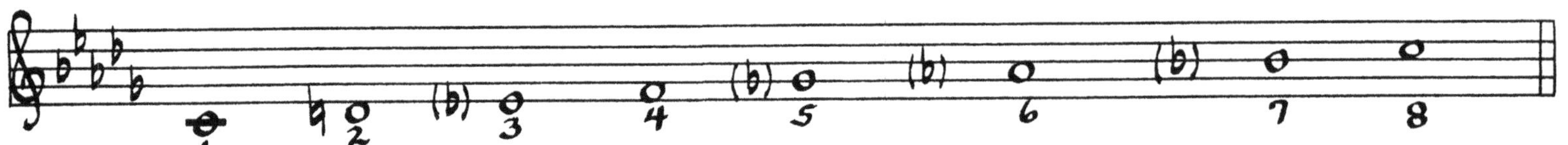

FINGERING

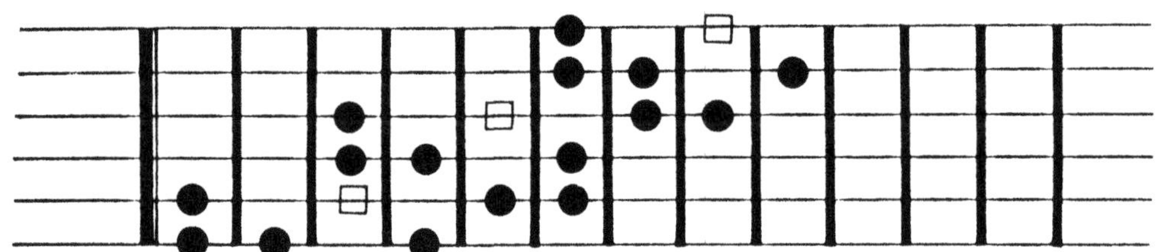

Four ways of conceiving a Locrian,#2 scale:

1. A pure minor scale with a lowered 5th scale step.
2. A Locrian scale having a raised 2nd scale step.
3. A Major scale with lowered 3rd, 5th, 6th, and 7th scale steps.
4. A scale that has the same tones as a melodic minor scale built on the note three half steps above. (C Locrian,#2 is the same as Eb melodic minor).

Application

The Locrian,#2 scale is used with a minor 7th chord having a lowered 5th (sometimes called a half-diminished chord). Such as Cm7b5. Any tone in the scale may be emphisezed.

When the unaltered 9th is present in the harmony, this scale would be a better choice then the pure Locrian mode, because the lowered 2nd scale step in the Locrian mode would sound off and clash to the 9th of the chord.

Locrian, ♯2 Scales

Super Locrian Scale

A scale of many names all correct and commonly used. The classical name is the Super Locrian scale. Heres the others, the Altered Dominant scale, the Pomeroy scale, the Ravel scale, and the Diminished Whole-Tone scale.
Constructed of 5 whole steps and 2 half steps. With the half steps occuring between steps 1 and 2 and steps 3 and 4 of the scale.

C Super Locrian

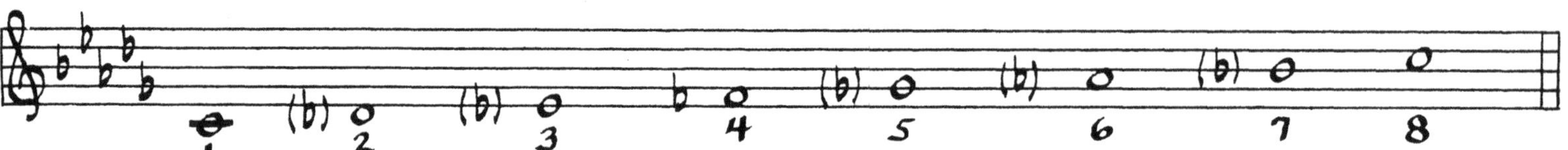

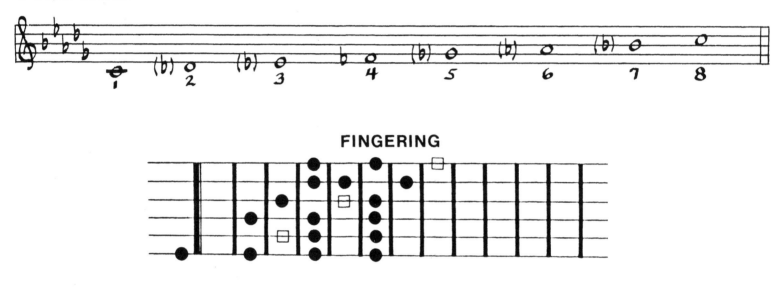

FINGERING

Two ways of conceiving a Super Locrian scale:

1. A Locrian scale with a lowered 4th scale step.
2. A scale that has the same tones as a melodic minor scale built on the note a half step above.

Application

The Super Locrian scale is used with dominant family chords, that have BOTH an altered 5th and an altered 9th in any combinationie, C7#5#9, C7b5#9, D7#5b9 C7b5b9. The chord may include both altered 5ths and both altered 9ths since all of these alterations occur as scale steps in the Super Locrian scale.

A whole tone or diminished scale might be a better choice if the dominant chord has NO altered 5th or 9th in it.

A Super Locrian scale has the same tones as a Lydian,b7 scale built on the note located a tri-tone above or below.

Super Locrian Scales

Jazz Minor Scale

One of the more common scales in the Jazz community referred to as the Jazz (or stright) Melodic Minor scale. The scale is formed by taking a Melodic Minor scale with the 6th and 7th steps raised BOTH ASCENDING AND DESCENDING.

"A" melodic scale

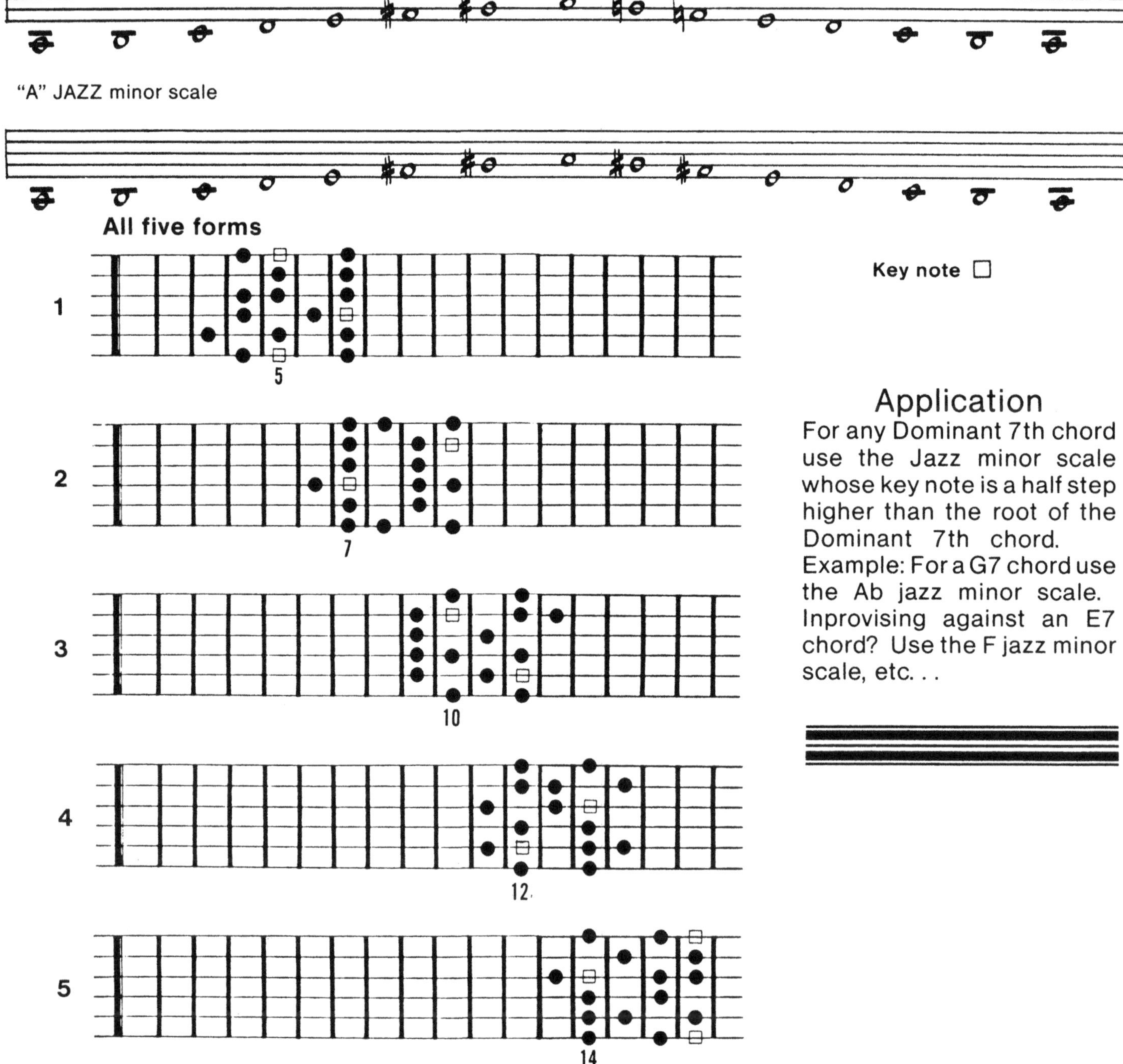

Application

For any Dominant 7th chord use the Jazz minor scale whose key note is a half step higher than the root of the Dominant 7th chord. Example: For a G7 chord use the Ab jazz minor scale. Inprovising against an E7 chord? Use the F jazz minor scale, etc. . .

Jazz (or straight) Melodic minor Scales

exercise based on the “A” Jazz minor scale

“D” Jazz minor scale fingering

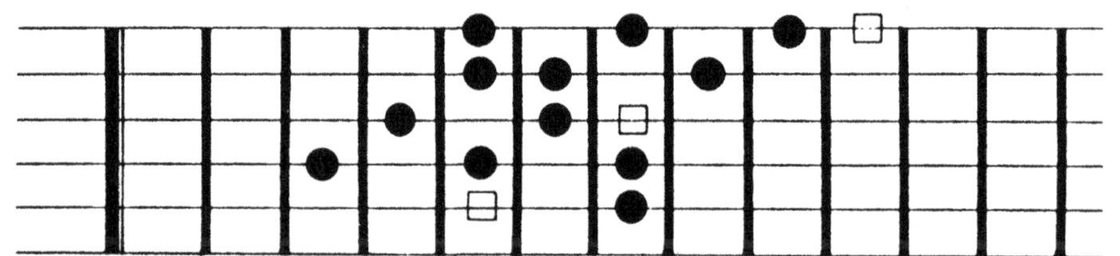

exercise based on the “D” Jazz minor scale

The Bop Scale
(Altered Mixolydian Mode)

This scale came into prominence during the Be Bop era and is one of the popular scales used today by jazz players. This scale is in reality a mixolydian mode with a half step added between the root and the 7th scale step.

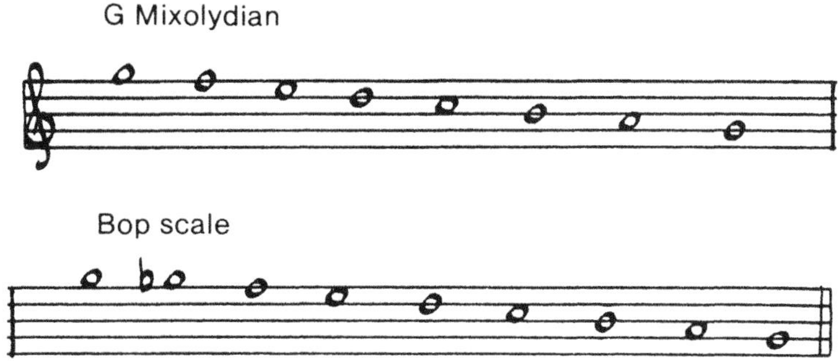

ADDING HALF STEPS TO MAJOR SCALES

Try adding half steps between the 5th and 6th scale tones of a major scale.

In the exercise below we start with a C maj.7 arpeggio (adding the half step between the 5th and 6th scale step) and moved into the BOP scale over the G7 chord.

PLAY UP AND DOWN THE FRETBOARD AND GOING TO THE LOWEST POSSABLE NOTE.

Quiz

Write the 3 scales in the staffs below. What do they all have in common? Answer on page-101

Ab Jazz minor

Db Lydian b7

G Super Locrian

Blues Scale

The Blues scale is constructed of 2 whole steps, 2 half steps,and 2 minor3rds. Location of the half steps and minor 3rds is shown below.

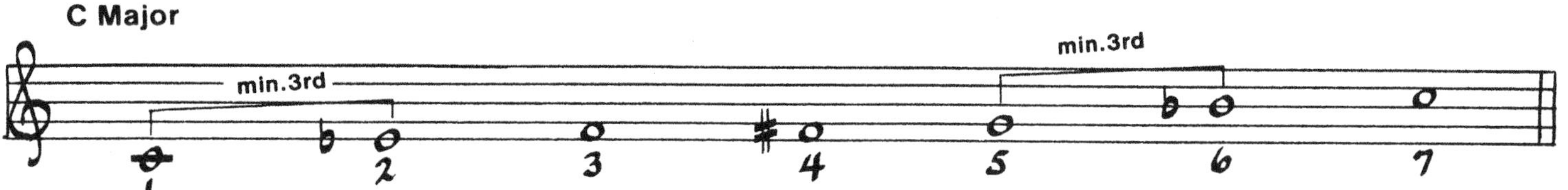

FINGERING

The Blues scale can be learned not by memorizing a whole new scale, but simply by learning a new note. From a minor pentatonic just insert the raised fourth.

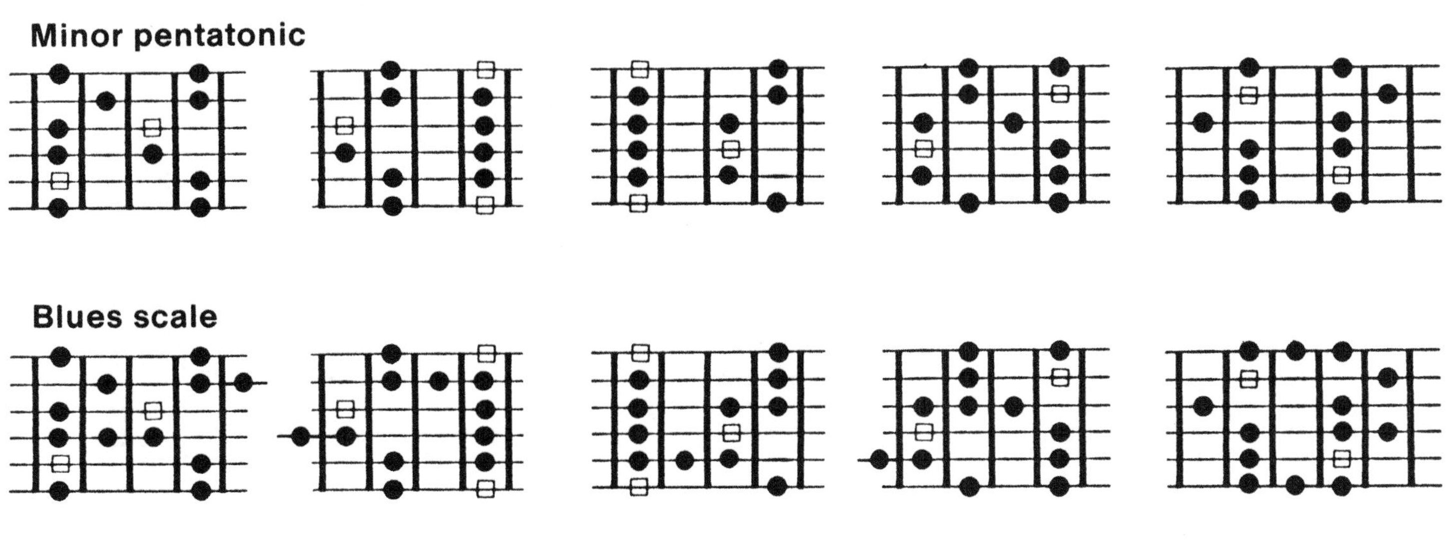

Application

The Blues scale like it's parent pentatonic scale is commonly used with both Minor and Dominant family chords.

When used with an unaltered minor 7th chord the natural 4th and the raised 4th can clash. The raised 4th has a tendency to resolve either up or down a half step to the 11th or 5th of the chord.

Used with a dominant chord, the 3rd scale tone is dissonant and wants to move away. The 2nd scale tone creates an augmented 9th in relation to the dominant harmony. This and the lowered 5th tends to give it the "BLUESY" quality.

The Blues scale is often used in conjunction with all 3 or 4 chords of a simple blues progression, in this case, ONLY THE BLUES SCALE BUILT ON THE TONIC NOTE OF THE KEY IS USED. (C blues scale in the key of C).

Since the blues scale is one of the most used member of the scale community. We pause on our road of scales to explore the Blues a little more.

Blues Scales

The Blues Scale Over Minor Chords

Like it's parent pentatonic scale, it can be used over minor harmony.

Lets use the G minor blues scale starting on the 3rd fret for this example.

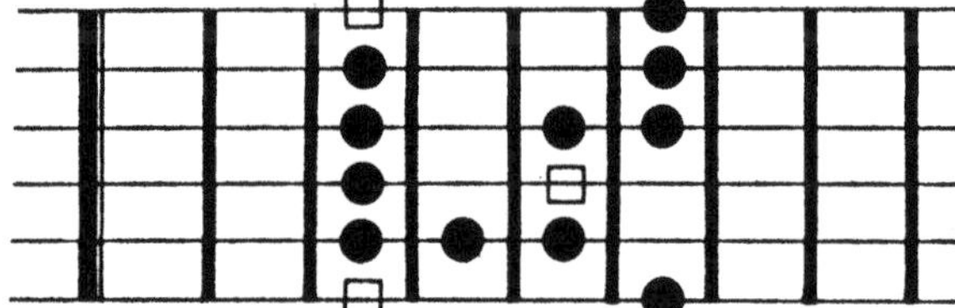

Write and play a blues line over this progression.

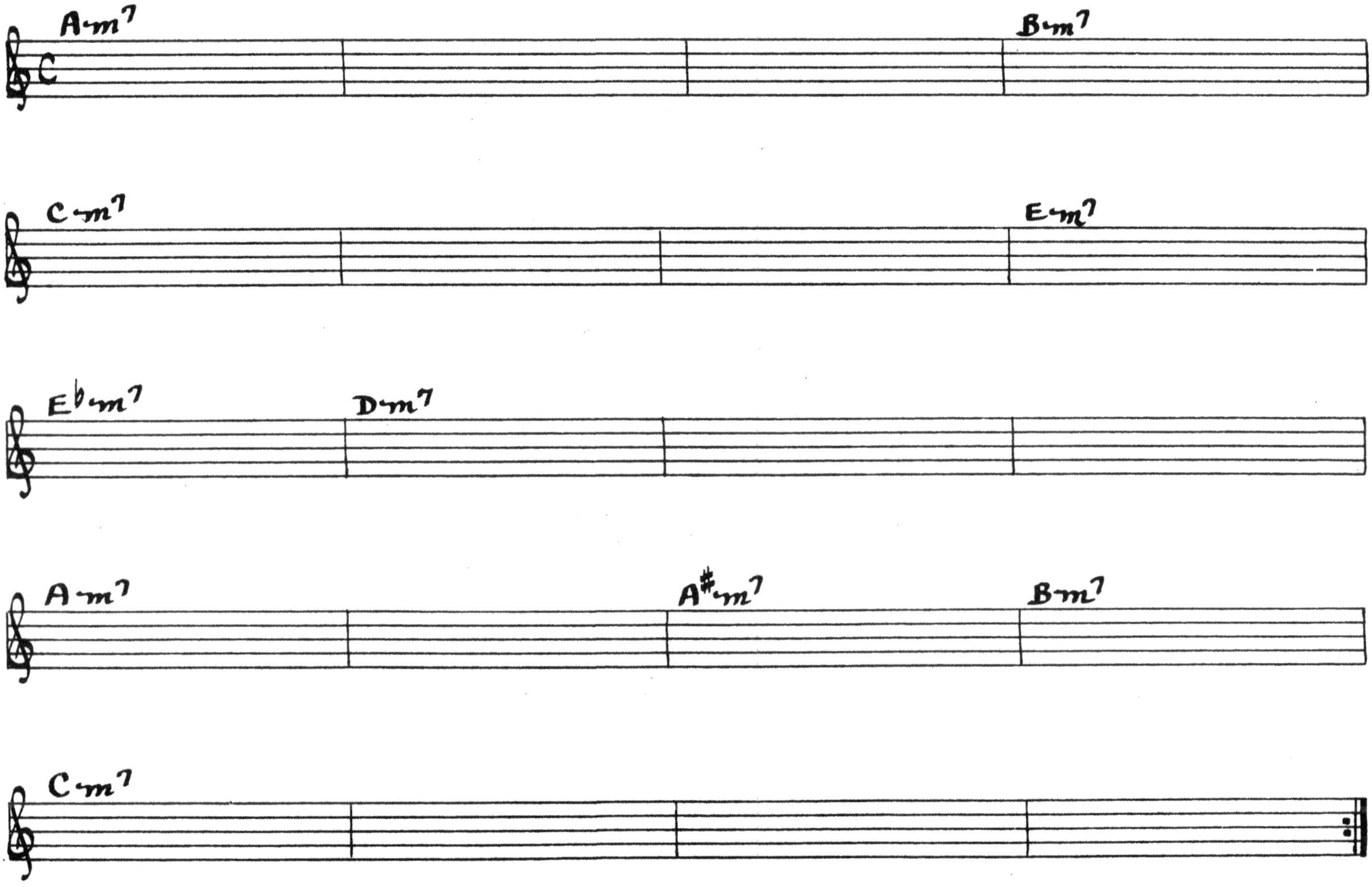

A-m7 B-m7

C-m7 E-m7

E♭-m7 D-m7

A-m7 A♯-m7 B-m7

C-m7

Blues Scale Over Dominant Chords

One of the nicest things about the blues scale is the fact that it can be used over the entire 12-bar blues progression.

In the Dominant chord progression below stay with the G blues scale on the 3rd fret for the first couple of trys, then try playing the same notes but in different positions around the fretboard. As you become familiar with the notes ALTER THE TIMING, play eight notes, dotted quarter, half notes etc.

Record or have a friend play the following progression and run through the scale. Try to make up a line as you go.

Blues Progressions

The basic 12 bar blues originally used what we call three chords. They were the Dominant 7ths built on the root, fourth and the fifth of the key you are in. Example: Key of G--G7,C7, D7. Key of A--A7, D7, E7. Key of E--E7, A7, B7, etc.

In the evolution of the blues with more and more musicians playing the "Three chord songs" naturally some would take liberties with the chord structure and even alter the chords. As various alterations were passed from player to player they eventually became part of the blues structure.

What follows on the next page is a list of 22 different 12 bar blues progressions. They read from left to right. As we move down and across, the progressions become more altered and more difficult. Feel free to create your own progressions. Or try substituting a bar or two from one progression to another one.

Number 18 is one that Charlie Parker used on a blues called "Blues For Alice" and one called "Laird Bird". Progression 20 uses a steady flow of minor chords moving to Dominant 7th chords. (the 11--V7 chord progression)

Listen to other players and see if you can hear when they are substituting chords, scales, licks or patterns over the basic three chord progression.

Listening to the ones who play the blues. That's the best way to learn.Guitarest like, Blind Lemon Jefferson, Lonnie Johnson, B.B. King, Eric Clapton, Reverend Gary Davis, Stefan Grossman, Robert Johnson, Son House, Muddy Waters, Duane Allman. Harp Players like Charlie Musslewhite, Mickey Raphael. Horn Players like Louis Armstrong and Kid Ory. And the list goes on and on . . . .

Blues Progressions

	Bar 1	2	3	4	5	6	7	8	9	10	11	12
1	G7	G7	G7	G7	C7	C7	G7	G7	D7	D7	G7	G7
2	G7	G7	G7	G7	C7	C7	G7	G7	D7	C7	G7	D7
3	G7	C7	G7	G7	C7	C7	G7	G7	A7	D7	G7	D7
4	G7	C7	G7	G7	C7	C7	G7	E7	A7	D7	G7	D7
5	G7	C7	G7	G7	C7	C7	G7	E7	Am7	D7	G7	Am7 D7
6	G7	C7	G7	G7	C7	F7	G7	E7	Eb7	D7	G7	Eb7 D7
7	G7	C7	G7	Dm7 G7	C7	F7	G7	Bm7 E7	Am7	D7	Bm7 E7	Am7 D7
8	G7	C7	G7	Dm7 G7	C7	F7	Bm7	E7	Am7	D7	Bm7 E7	Am7 D7
9	G7	C7	G7	Dm7 G7	C7	C#dim	G7	E7	Am7	D7	G7 E7	Am7 D7
10	G7	C7	G7	Dm7 G7	C7	C#m7 F#7	G7 Gb7	F7 E7	Am7	D7 C7	Bm7 E7	Am7 D7
11	G7	C7	G7	Dm7 G7	C7	Cm7	Bm7	E7	Am7	D7	G7 E7	Am7 D7
12	Gmaj7	F#7 B7	Em7 A7	Dm7 G7	C7	Cdim7	Bm7 E7	Bbm7 Eb7	Am7 D7	Ebm7 Ab7	G7 E7	Am7 D7
13	Gmaj7	Am7 Bbdim7	Bm7	Dm7 G7	C7	Cm7 F9	Bm7	Bbm7	Am7	D7	G7 E7	Am7 D7
14	Gmaj7	F#7 Fm7	Em7 Ebm7	Dm7 Db7	Cmaj7	Cm7	Bm7	Bbm7	Am7	D7	Bbm7 Bm7	Am7 Ab7
15	Gmaj7	Cmaj7	Bm7 Am7	Abm7 C#7	Cmaj7	Cm7	Bm7	Bbm7	Am7	Abm7	Gmaj7 Bbm7	Am7 Ab7
16	Gmaj7	F#m7b5 B7	Em7 A7	Dm7 G7	Cmaj7	Cm7 F9	Bbmaj7	Bbm7 Eb9	Am7	Am11 Ab7b5	G7 E7#9	Am7 D7b9
17	Gmaj7	Cmaj7	Bm7 Am7	Abm7 C#7	Cmaj7	Cm7 F7	Bbmaj7	Bbm7 Eb7	Abmaj7	Am7 D7	Bm7 E7	Ebm7 Ab7
18	Gmaj7	F#m7 B7	Em7 A7	Dm7 G7	Cmaj7	Cm7 F7	Bm7	Bbm7 Eb7	Am7	D7	Bm7 E7	Am7 D7
19	Gmaj7	Fm7 B7	Em7 A7	Abm7 C#7	Cmaj7	C#m7 F#7	Bm7	Bbm7 Eb7	Am7	D7 C#7	Bm7 E7	Am7 D7
20	G#m7 C#7	F#7 B7	Em7 A7	Dm7 G7	Cmaj7	Cm7 F7	Bbmaj7	Bbm7 Eb7	Abmaj7	Am7 D7	Bm7 E7	Am7 D7
21	Gmaj7	G#m7 C#7	F#maj7 Fmaj7	Ebmaj7 C#maj7	Cmaj7	C#m7 F#7	Bmaj7	Bm7 E7	Amaj7	Abmaj7	Gmaj7 Bbmaj7	Amaj7 Ab
22	Abm7 Db7	F#m7 B7	Em7 A7	Dm7 G7	Cmaj7	Cm7 F9	Bbmaj7	Bbm7 Eb9	Abmaj7	Am7 D7	Gmaj7 Bb13	A13 Ab13

G Arpeggio Type Blues

Rhythm chords for the above arpeggio style blues be-bop exercise in the key of G. Chords in parenthesis are the basic progression. The others are substitute chords to create melodic movement.

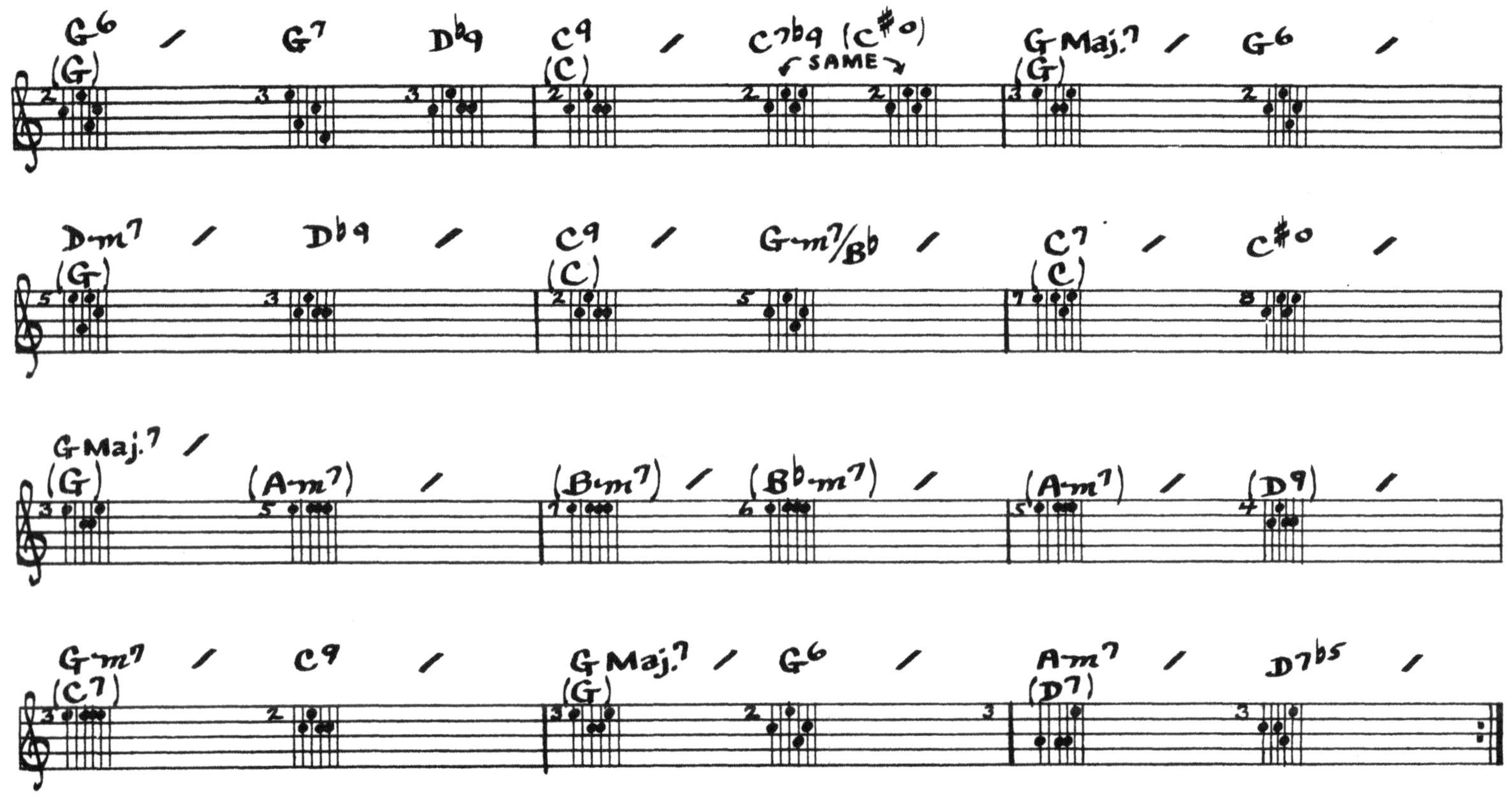

(this page is a gift from George Ports.....thanks Chief)

Answer to page 92

Notice that all three scales have the SAME notes in them? Just with a different Key or Tonic note. These three scales all come from the JAZZ MINOR SCALE in the same way the Dorian, Lydian or Mixolydian etc. come from the major scale.

The G Super Locrian mode is built from the 7th note of the Jazz minor scale, therefor the G super locrain can be used against a G7 chord as it comes from and contains the same notes as the Ab Jazz minor scale.

The Db Lydian,b7 is built on the 4th note of the Ab jazz minor scale so it too could be used against that same G7 chord.

The thought is this: same scales just fancy names, learn to use then, with a through understanding of the CONSTRUCTION and APPLICATIONS of scales, YOU can make them what they should be: a help rather then a hindrance.

Arpeggios

Don't skip over this subject!

I know you're saying "What's arpeggios got to do with being a great Rock and Roll star, or playing on a recording date?"

Arpeggios are not the most popular thing to do on the guitar, maybe because they are probably the HARDEST musical exercises to play well, on the guitar. A horn player or keyboardist can play chord arpeggios the likes of which we only dream about, perhaps because they are part of their daily practice routine and for us guitarists' no one teaches them to us plus most books don't even mention them. Well, the fact is most guitarists who don't play or know about arpeggios will have a blind spot in their playing and it soon shows up. So lets get started....Simply stated, an arpeggio are the notes of a chord played not simultaneously, but in rapid succession---broken or spread out.

Improvising often combines the use of scale tones and arpeggios and we show a wide variety of ways in this section. Play them all and stay with the ones you like. Of course these are all movable patterns and should be played up and down the fretboard.

Arpeggiated Triads

C chord **C Arpeggio**

The major triad comes from the first, third and fifth notes of the major scale.

C Major

Use this form to play the arpeggio patten below.

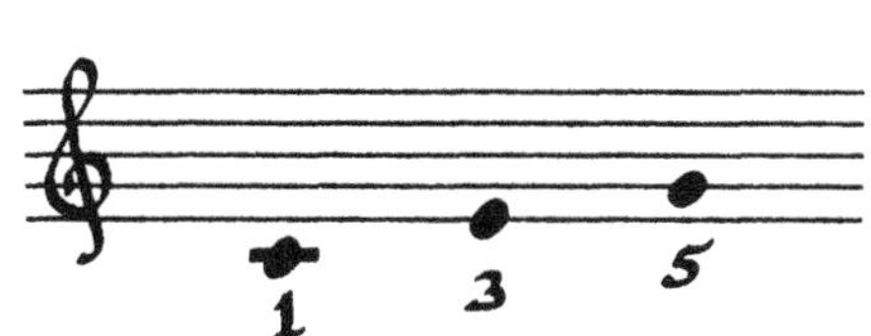

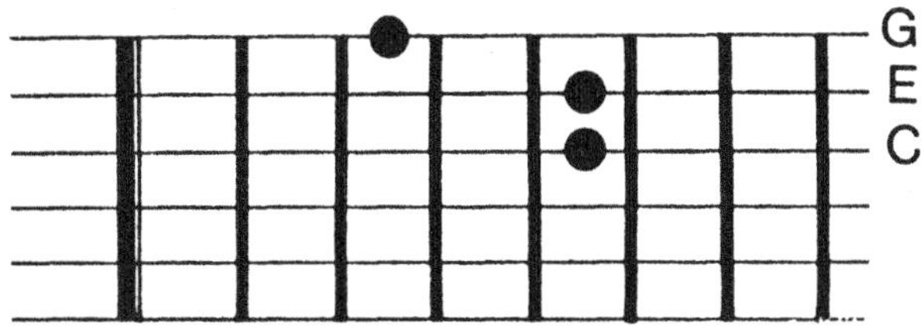

Example I

C Minor

Using the 1, 3, 5th of the major scale, we just FLAT the 3rd note ONE FRET.

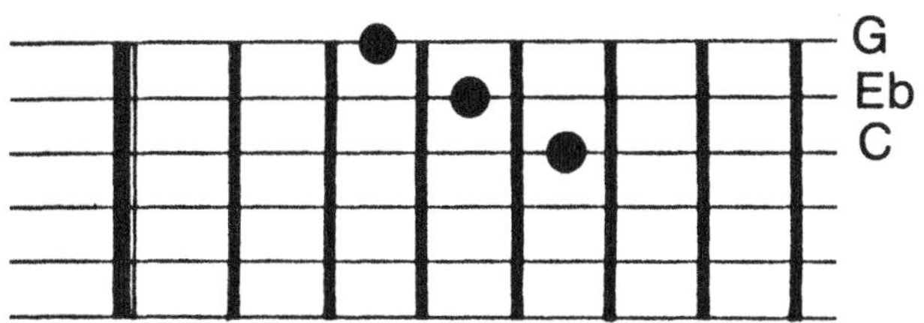

Use this form and play the pattern of example 1 again (remember, we flat the 3rd note, Eb).

C Augmented

Using the 1, 3, 5 of the major scale we raised the 5th note one fret G to G#.

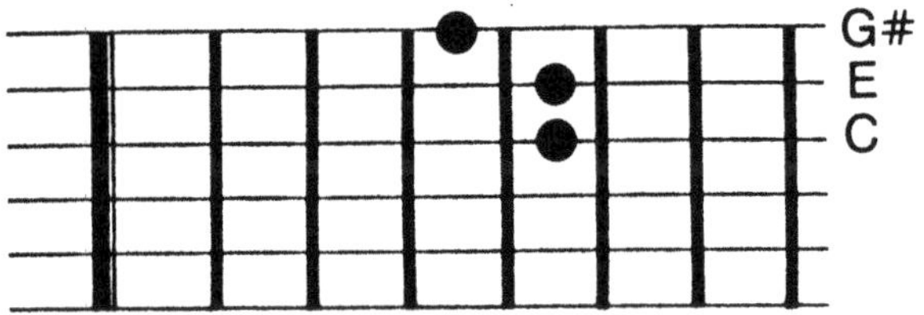

Use this form and again play the pattern of example 1.

C Diminished

Again using the 1, 3, 5 of the major scale we flat the 3rd-E to Eb and 5th-G to Gb.

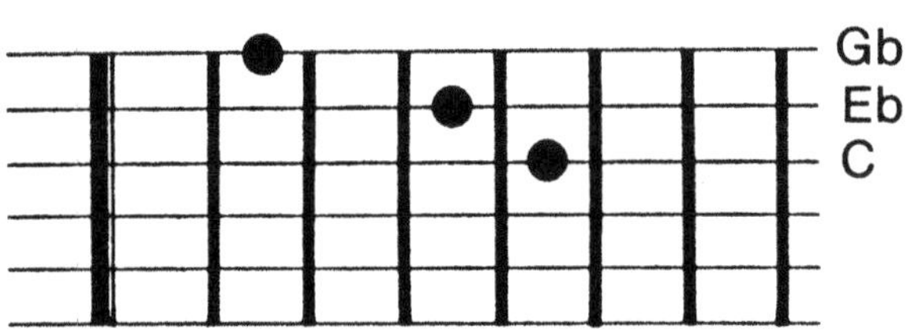

Use this form and play example 1 again remember the 3rd and 5th are flatted.

Practice this exersice using the arpeggios you've just learned.

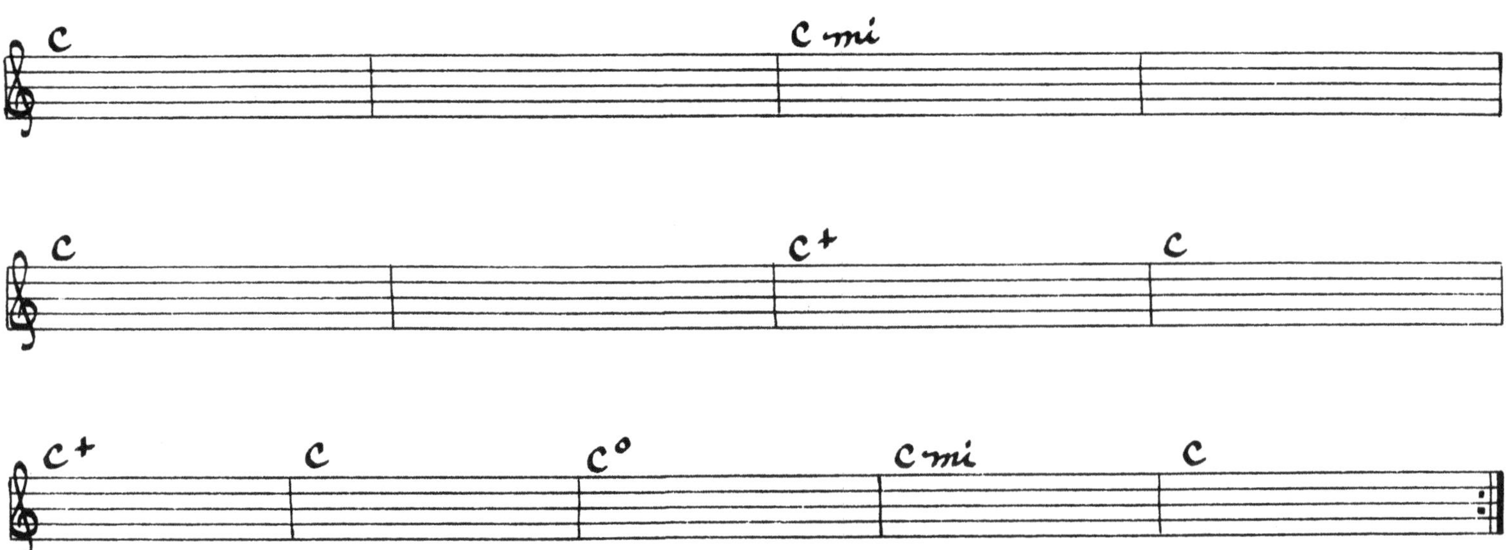

Arpeggiated Triads

using the "D" major scale

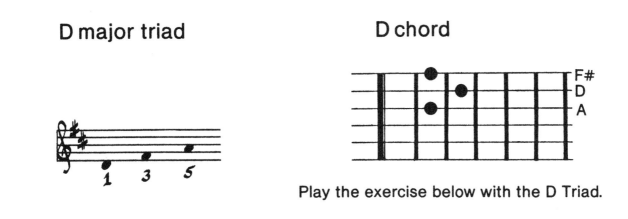

D major triad

D chord

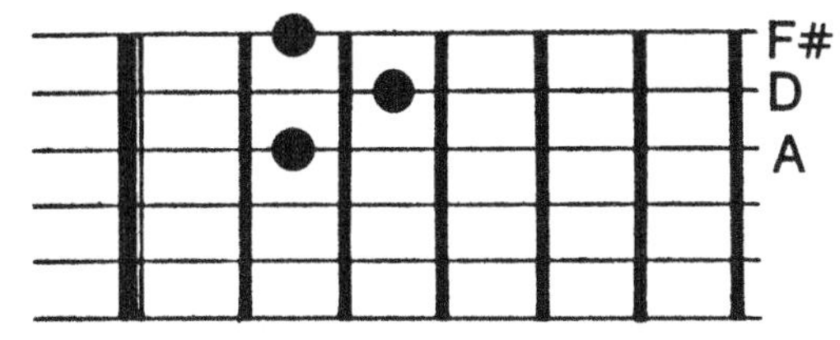

Play the exercise below with the D Triad.

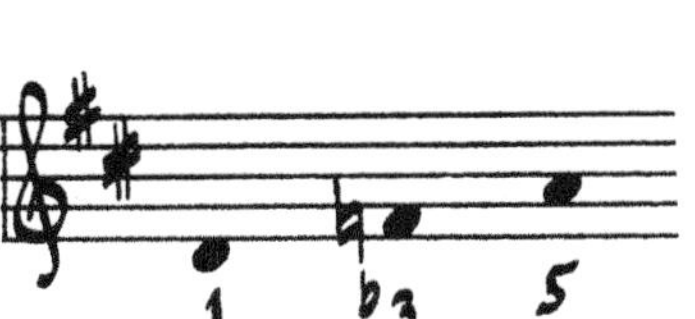
D minor triad

D minor chord

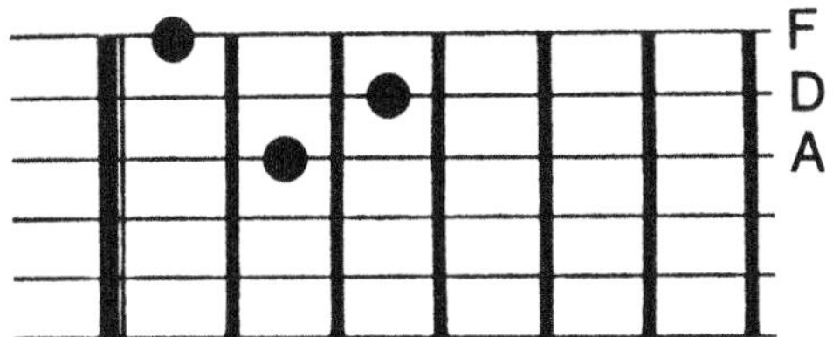

Play the exercise below with the D Minor Triad

D augmented triad

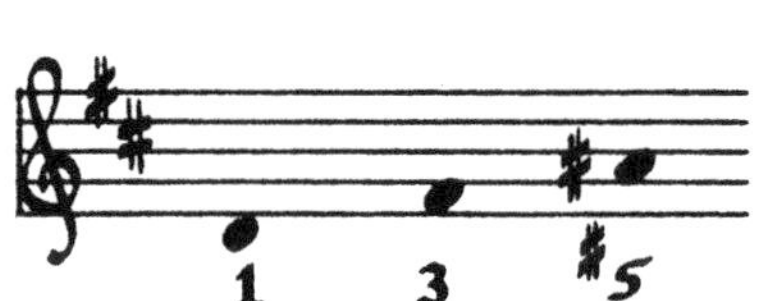

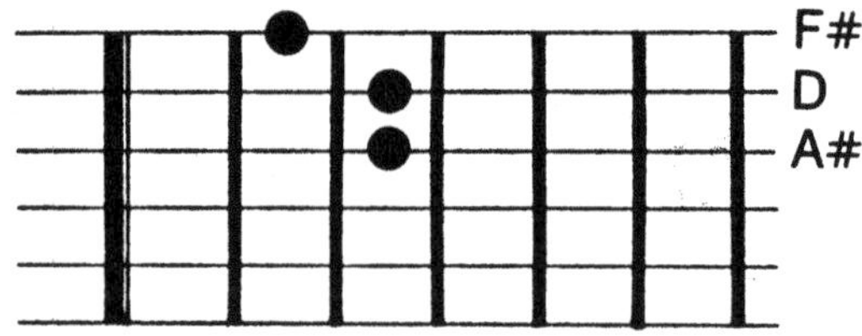

Play the exercise below with the D aug triad.

D Diminished Triad

D dim Chord

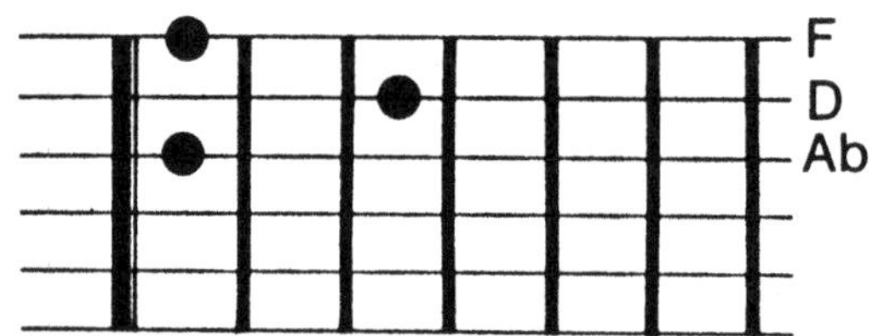

Practice this exercise using all the D triads you've just learned

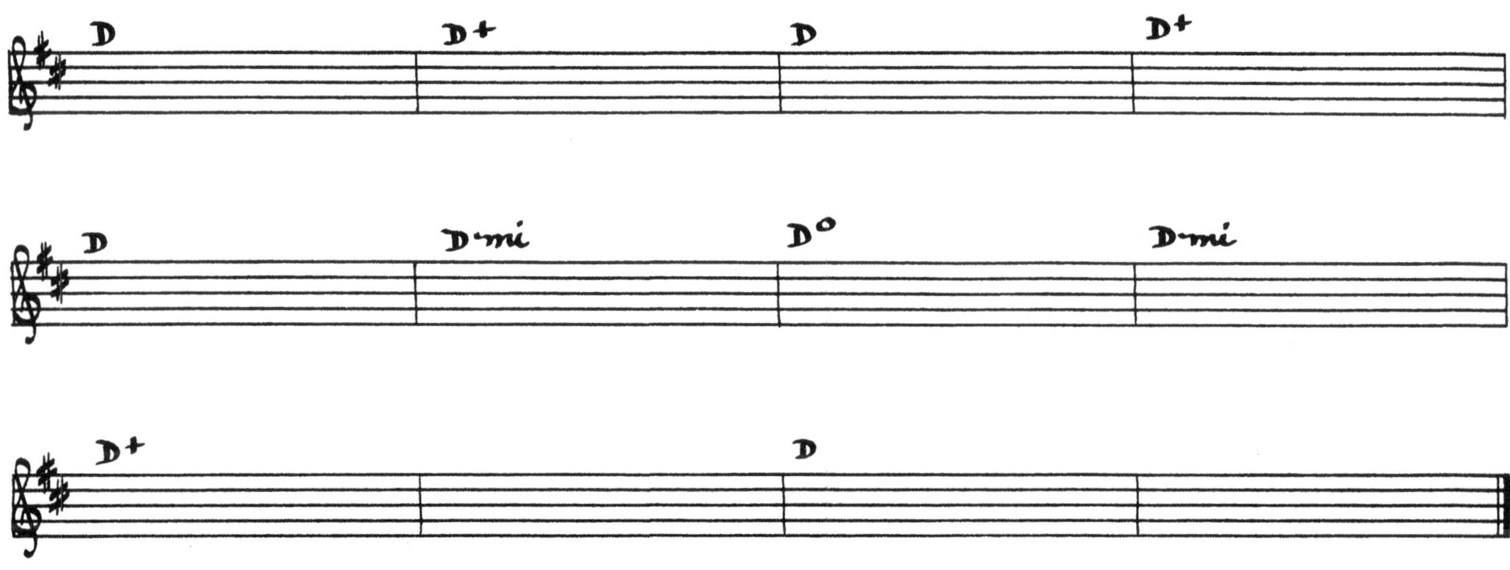

Arpeggios From The Major Harmonic Scale

These arpeggios are based on the G major Diatonic scale, on each degree (or scale step) we·ve build a chord simply by adding thirds on top of each note, See example below.

Gmaj 7 arpeggio

Gmaj 7 chord

Am 7 arpeggio

Am 7 chord

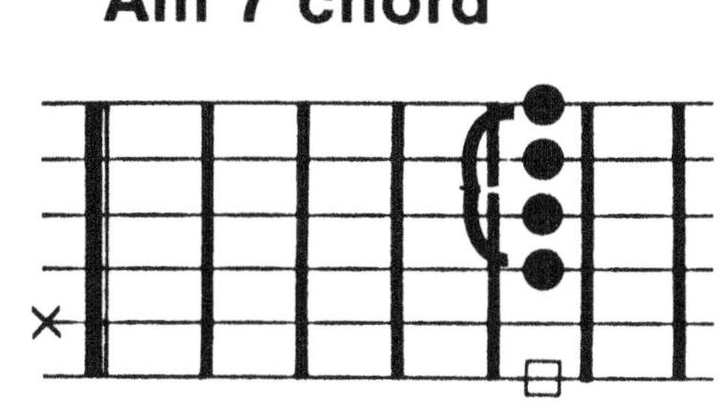

Bm 7 arpeggio

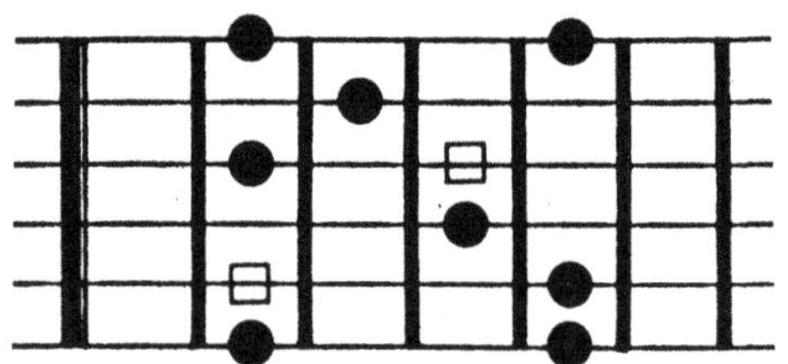

Bm 7 chord

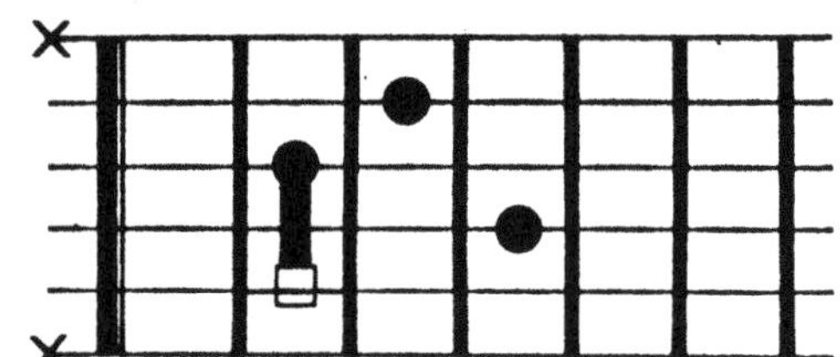

Cmaj 7 arpeggio

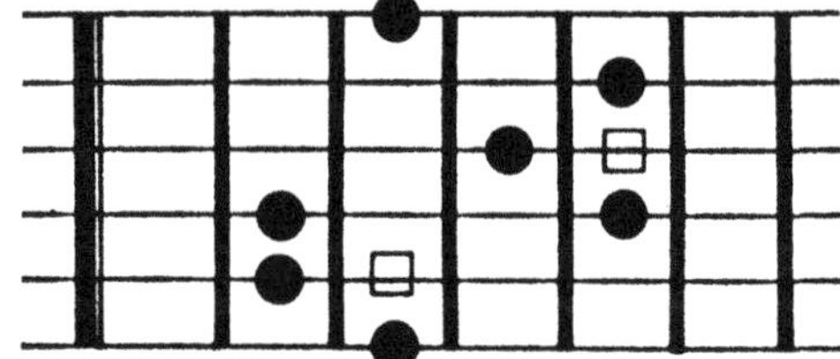

Cmaj 7 chord

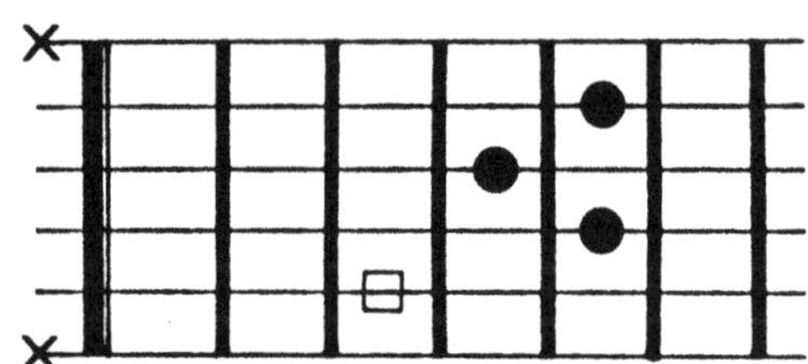

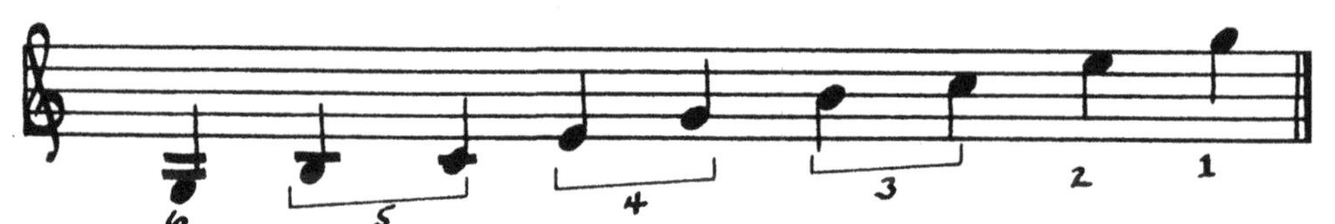

D7 arpeggio

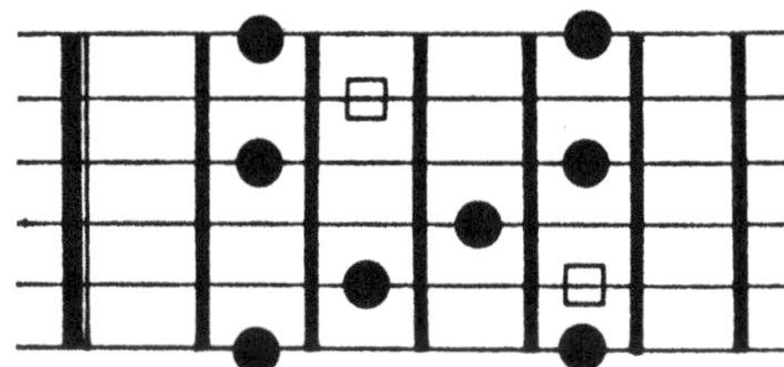

D7 chord

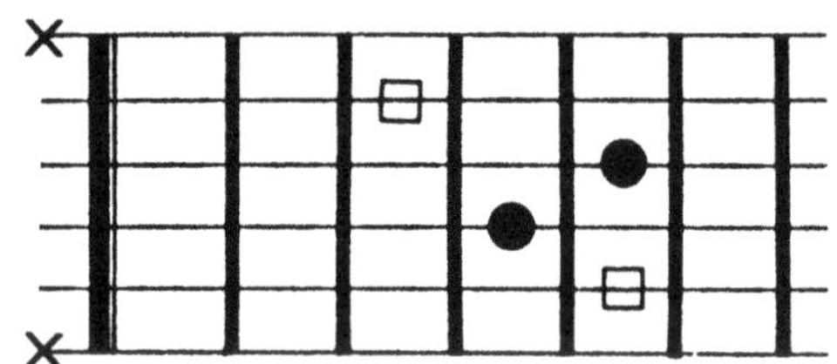

Em 7 arpeggio

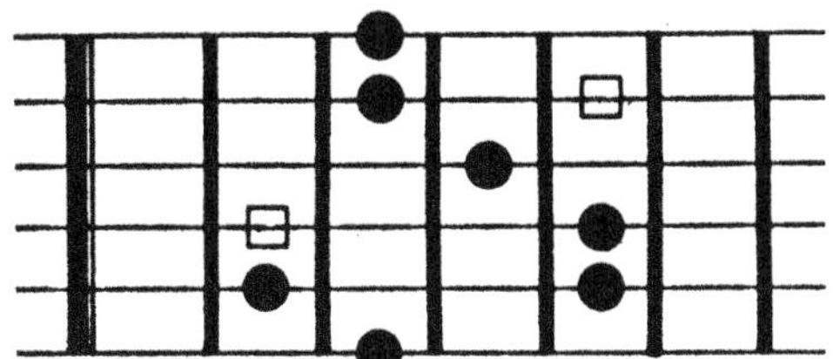

Em 7 chord

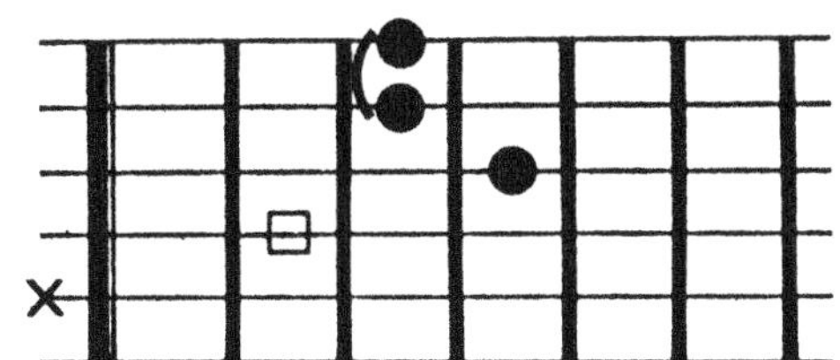

F#m 7-5 arpeggio

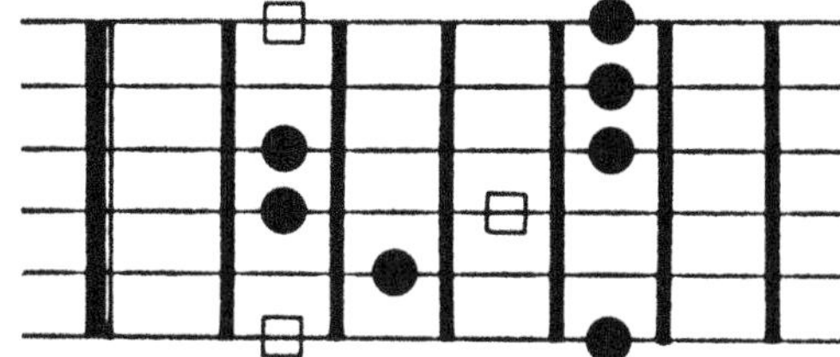

F#m 7-5 chord

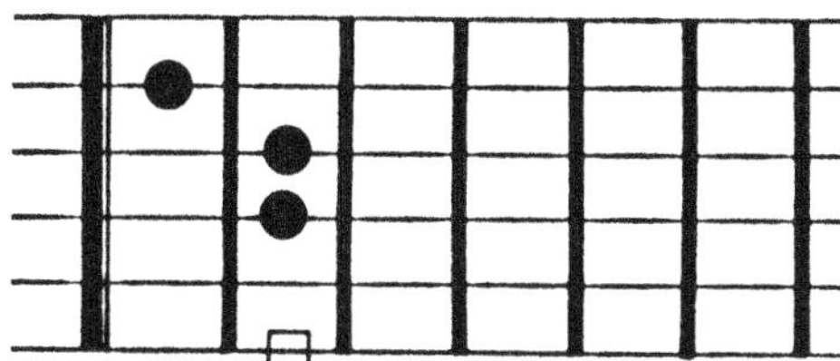

"You're not in control if you have to constantly calculate the applications of scales to chords throughout a solo. They should become second nature so that if there is any change in the harmonic territory you're improvisation can be easily handled, without losing sight of the whole structure of the solo".

Arpeggio fingering and exercises for the II, V, I chord in the key of C.

We already know the fingering for the I or major 7th chord, in case you need a review it's shown below.

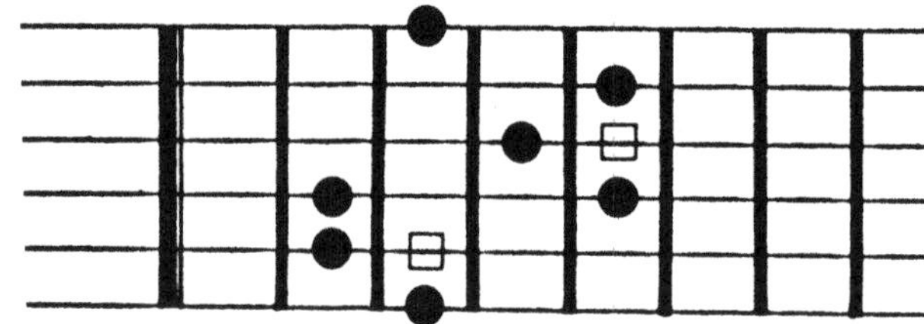

Based on the I chord, the major 7th start on the 6th string, 3rd fret G and play up the fretboard.

This next set of exercises has us playing around on the notes of the arpeggio still staying with only the major 7th arpeggio, as with the last exercise you should play this up and down the fretboard.

The I chord is often changed to a major 6th or major 9th chord. So let's play those arpeggios.

In this set of exercise we add the 6th and 9th steps increasing the melodic possibilities.

The 2 Chord Arpeggio

The II chord in the major scale is a minor 7 derived from the Dorian Mode. See page 38 for more information on the Dorian Mode.

Below is the D minor 7 scale (or D dorian mode) based on our original C major scale.

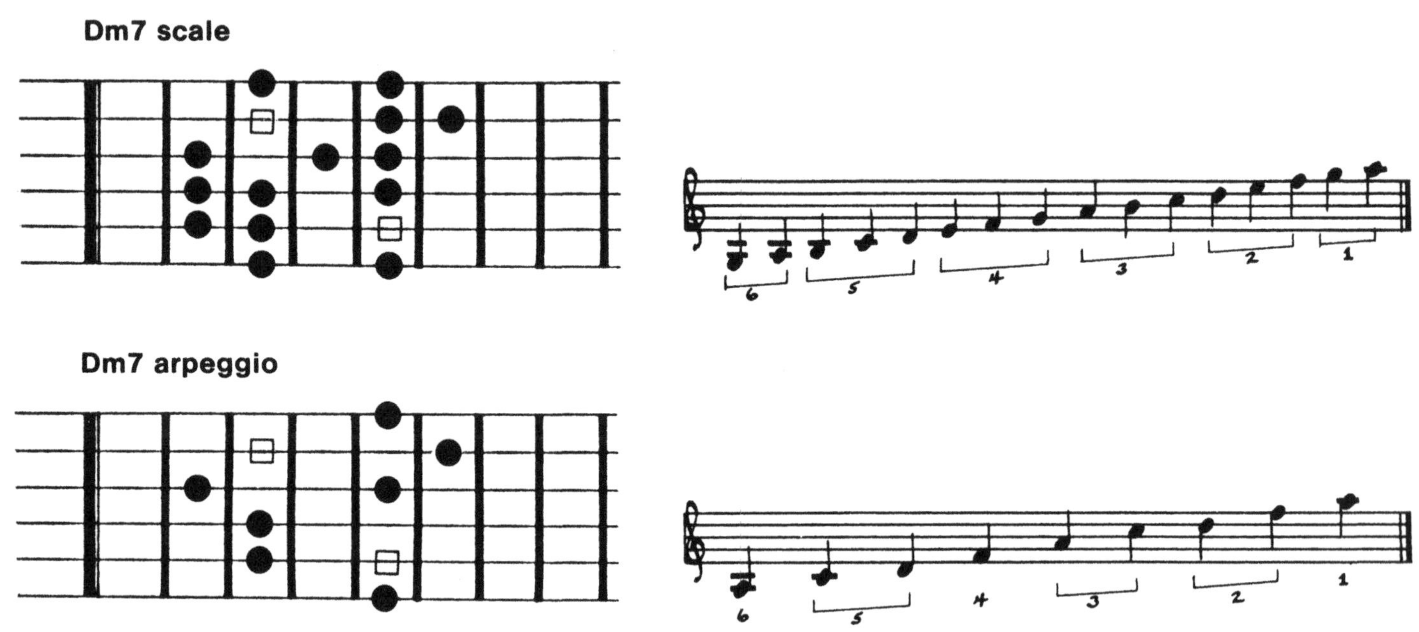

Based on the 2 chord the minor 7th this exercise begins with the Dm7 in the key of C and moves up by half steps up the fretboard.

Exercises Using The 2 Chord Arpeggio

This exercise is based on only the notes of the Dm7 arpeggio. Play up the fretboard.

Dm7 chord can also be extended to a minor 9th chord. Below is the Dm9 chord arpeggio fingering.

Dm9 arpeggio

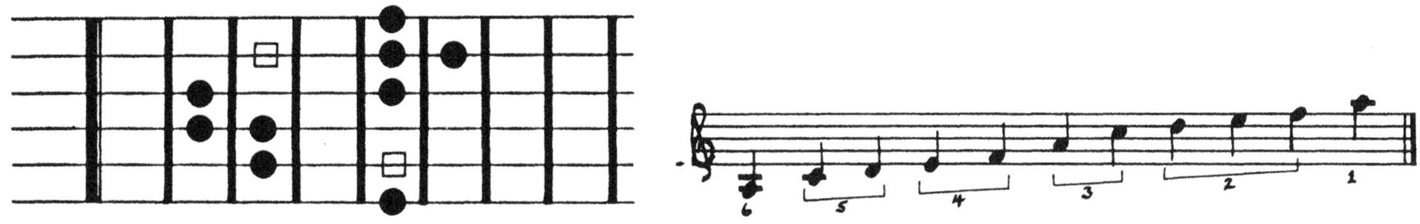

Adding again the 6th and 9th to the chord increases the melodic possibilities.

The 5 Chord Arpeggio

The 5 chord in the Major scale is a Dominant 7th, derived from the Mixolydian mode, see page 47 for additional information on the Mixolydian mode.

Below is our G7 scale (or Mixolydian mode) based on our original C scale.

G7 scale

G7 arpeggio

Exercises Using The 5 Chord Arpeggio

Based on the 5 chord, the Dominant 7th, This exercise begins with the G7 in the key of C moving in half-steps up the fretboard.

This exercise is based on only the notes of the G7 arpeggio. Play up the fretboard.

G9 arpeggio

Adding the 9th note (A)

G13 arpeggio

Adding the 6th (13th) and 9th notes (Eand A).

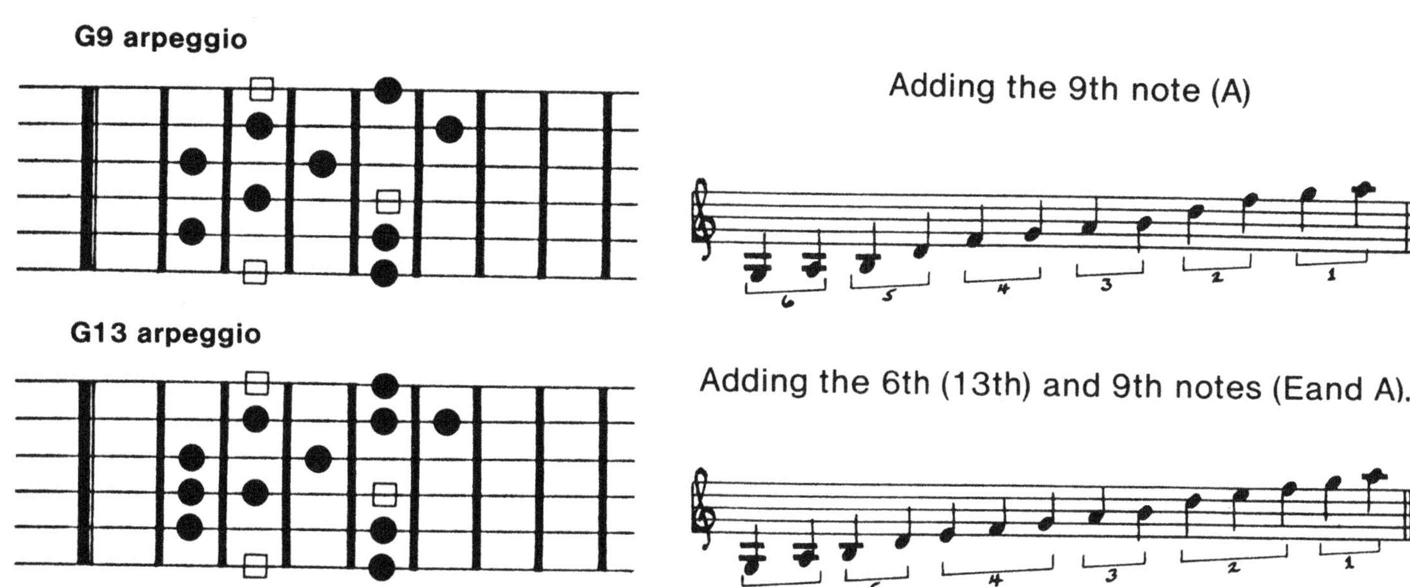

Two exercises adding the 6th (13th) and 9th notes.

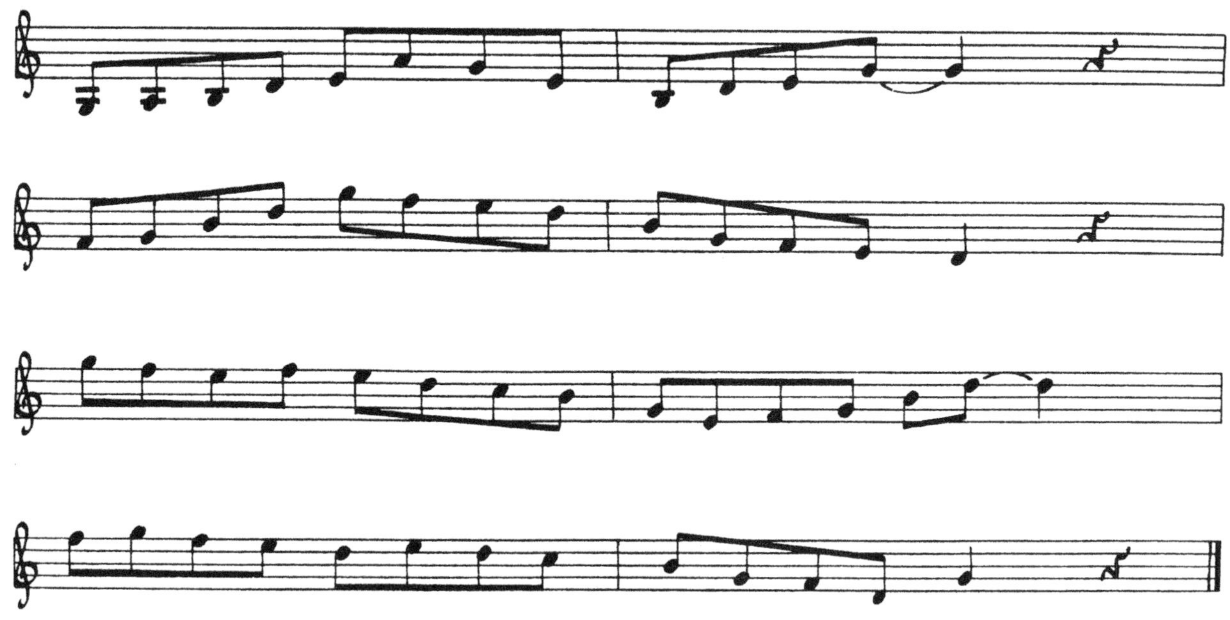

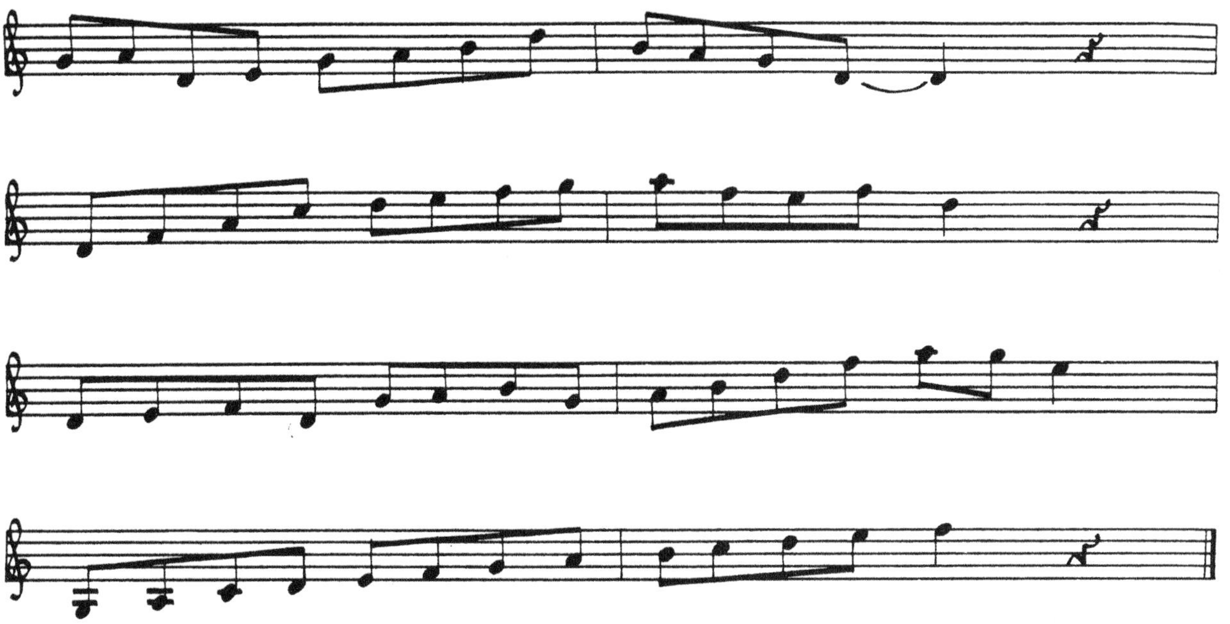

Alternate fingering for the II, V, I chord arpeggios in the key of D

Using the II, V, I chords these arpeggios are based on the D major scale shown below.

The I Chord

D major scale

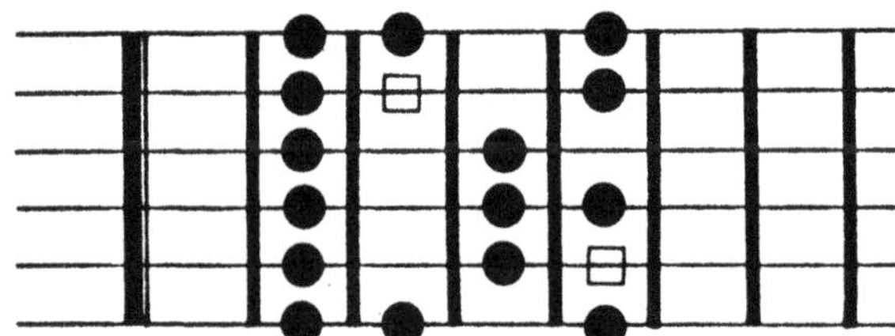

In order to make full use of all the notes available to us in the chord, we go below the root to the sixth string.

D maj 7 arpeggio

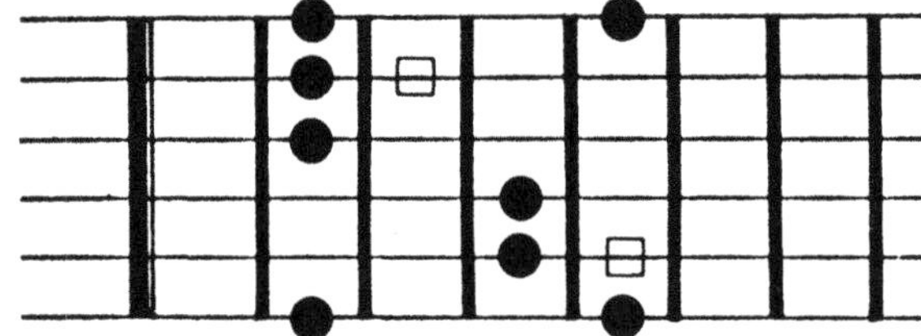

D6 arpeggio

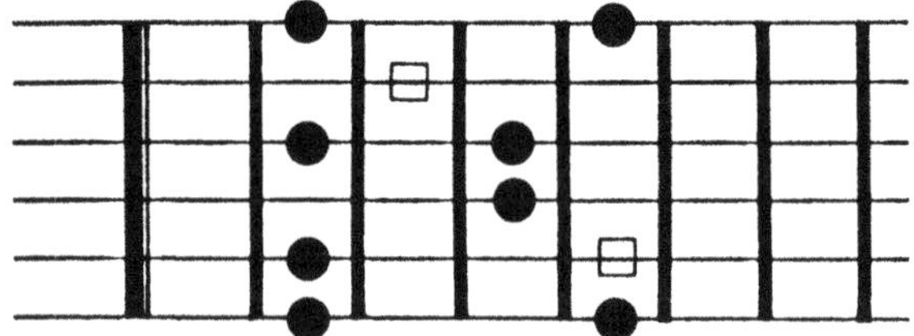

Adding the 6 (or 13) scale step (B)

D maj 9 arpeggio

Adding the 9th scale step (E)

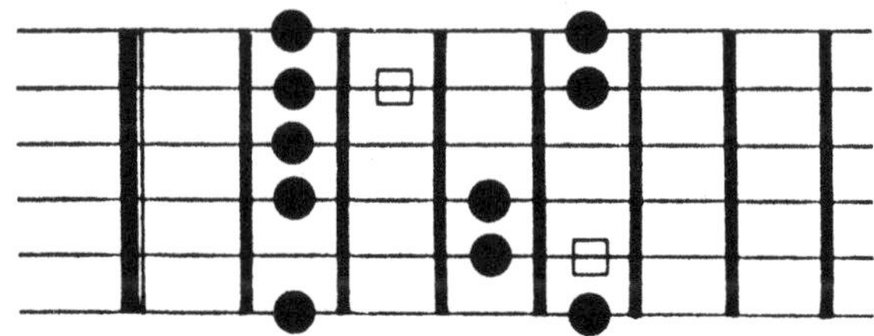

The II Chord

The II chord is based on the E Dorian mode or Em7 scale.

E Dorian(Em7 scale)

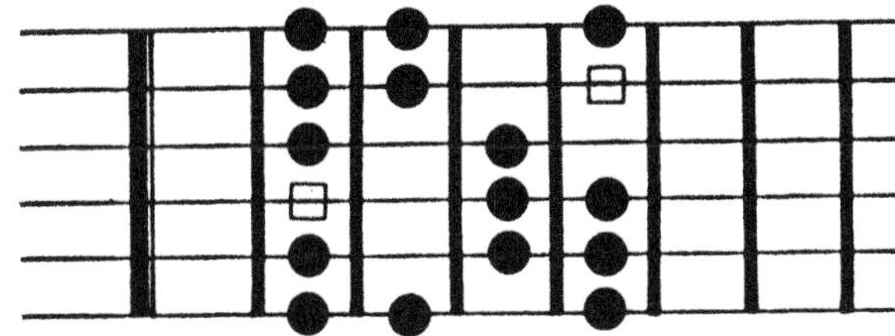

Em7arpeggio

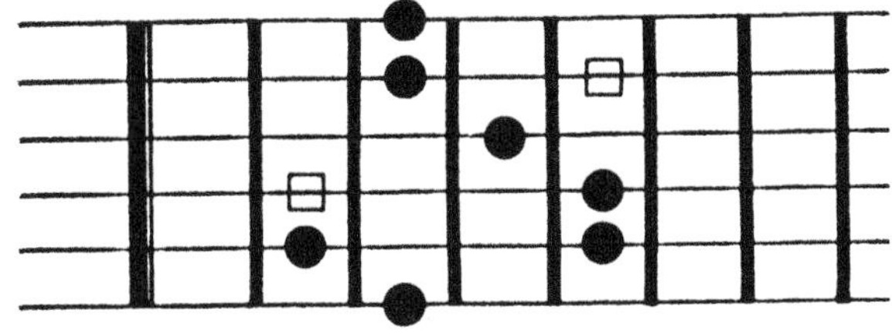

Also adding the 9th scale step (F#) making a Em9 chord

Em9 arpeggio

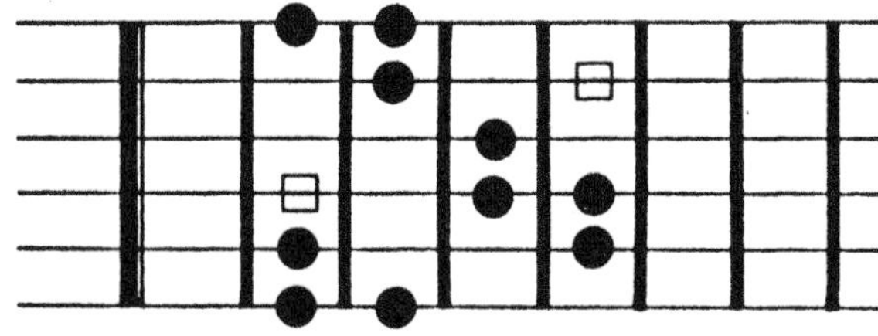

"As we play the scales we should be able to name each note and it's relationship to the chord,.....root, 3rd, 5th, 7th etc"

The V Chord

The V chord is based on the A Mixolydian mode, called the Dominant 7th chord.

A mixolydian (dominant 7th scale)

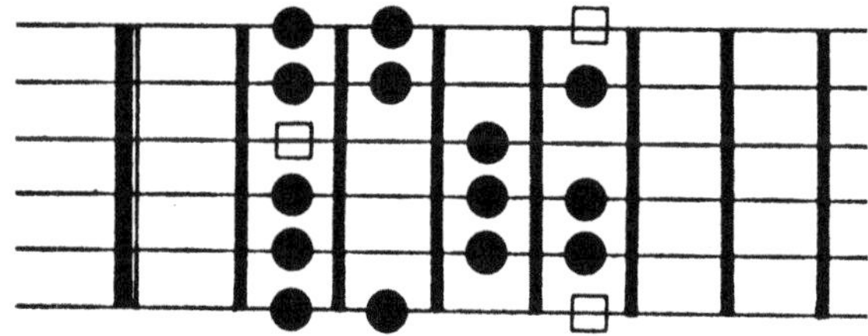

A7 arpeggio

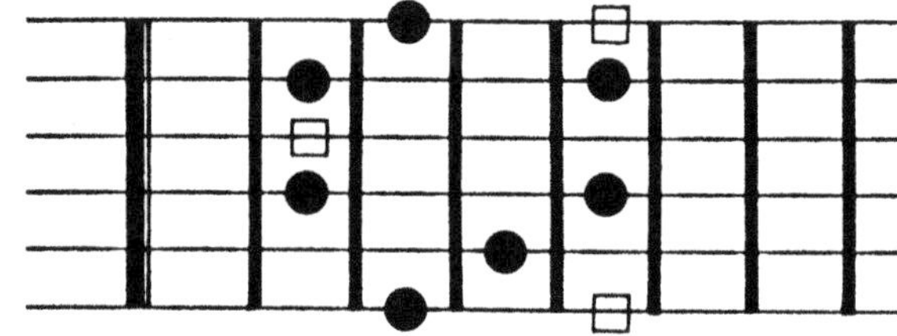

A9 arpeggio

Adding the 9 scale step (B)

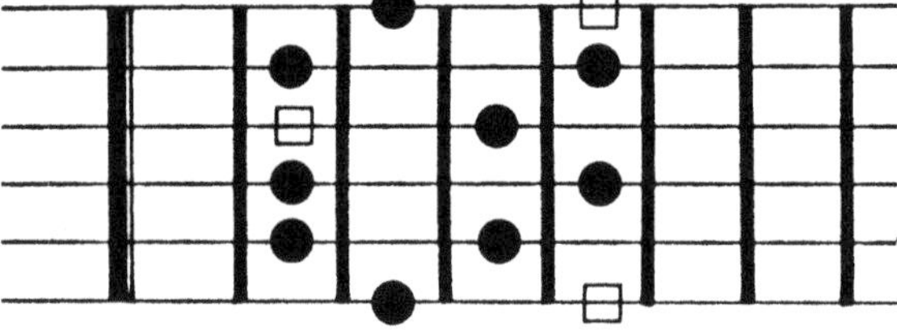

A13 arpeggio

Adding the 6 (or 13) scale step (F#)

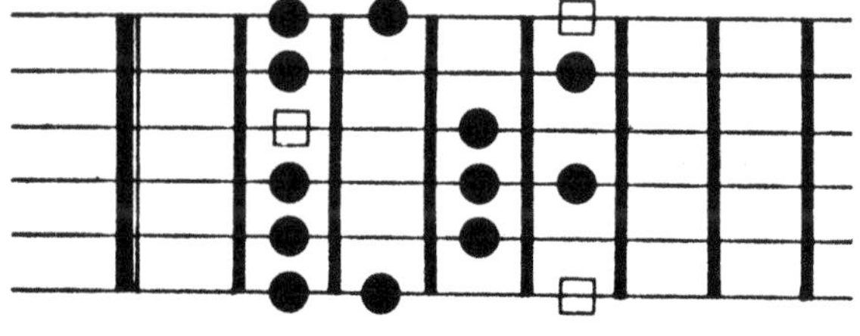

Alternate fingering for the II, V, I chord arpeggios in the key of A

Using the II, V, I, chords, these arpeggios are based on the A Major scale shown below.

The I chord

A major

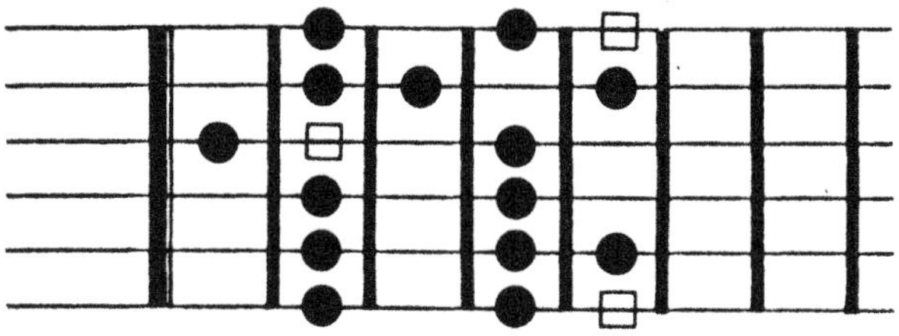

Amaj7 arpeggio

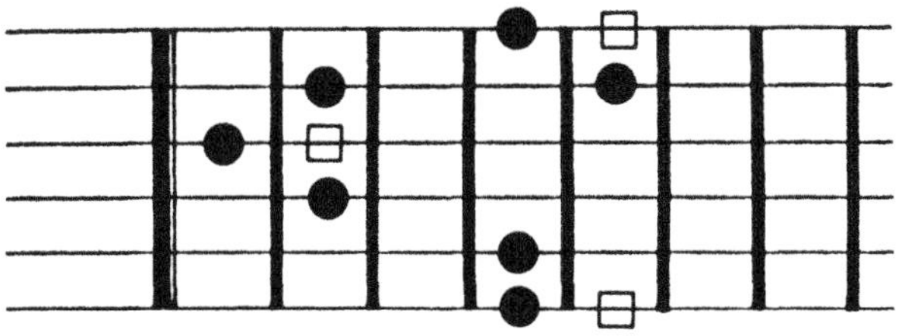

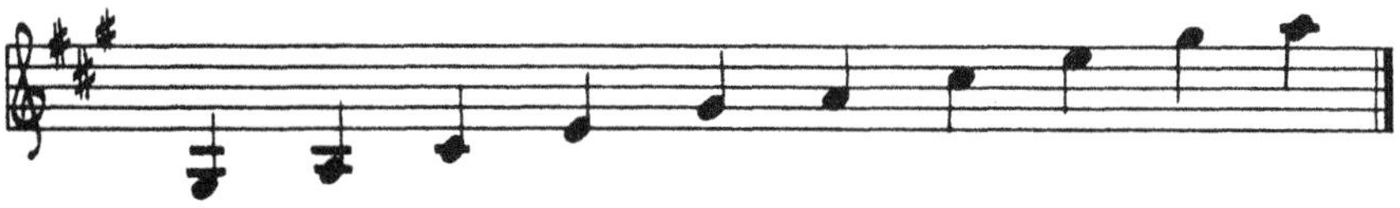

A6 arpeggio

Adding the 6th (or 13th) scale step (F#)

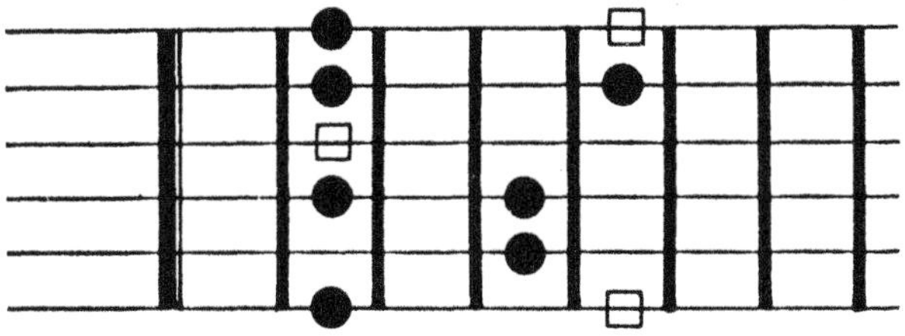

A maj 9 arpeggio

Adding the 9th scale step (B)

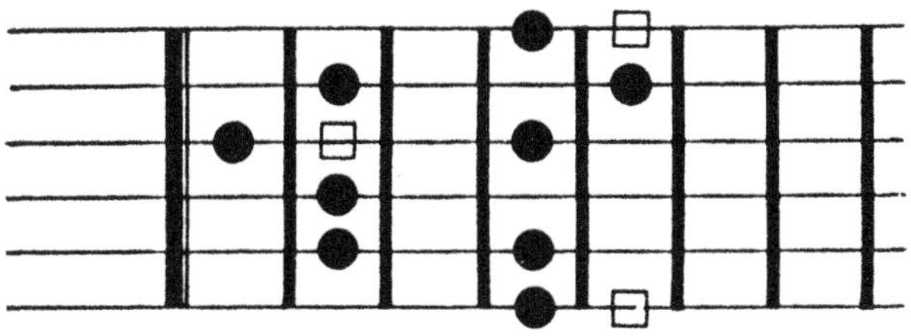

The II Chord

The II chord is based on the B Dorian mode or Bm7 scale

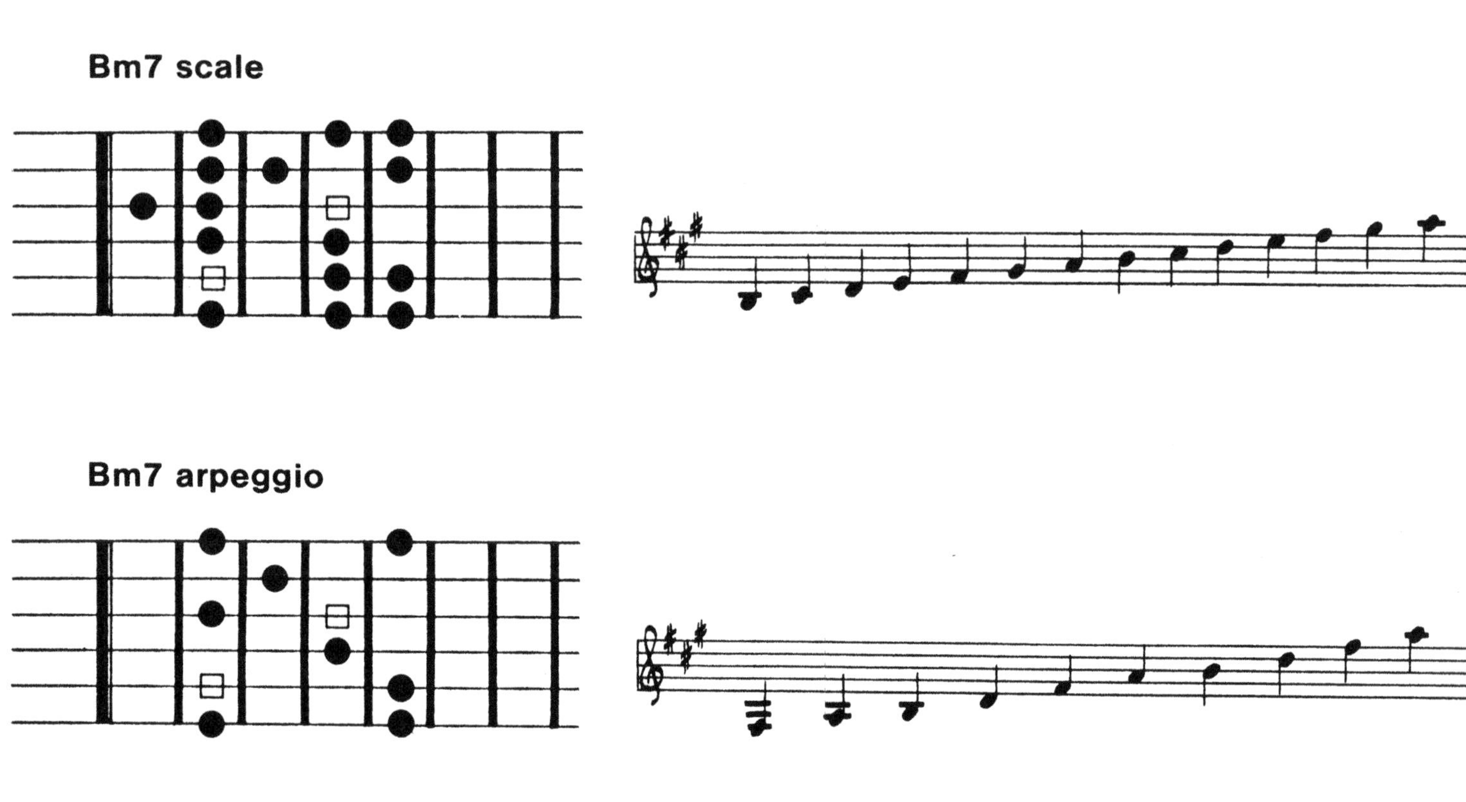

Also adding the 9th scale step (C#) making a Bm9 chord

"If you practice the wrong thing or the wrong way it's learned just like the right way and it's harder to move out"

The V Chord

The V chord is based on the E Mixolydian mode, called the Dominant 7th chord.

E Mixolydian (Dominant 7th) scale

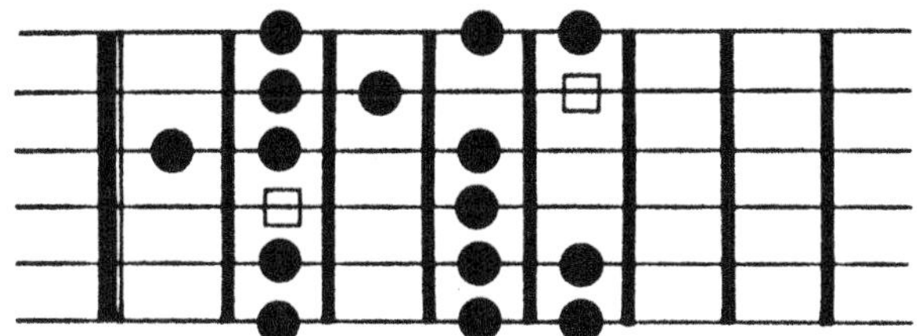

E7 arpeggio

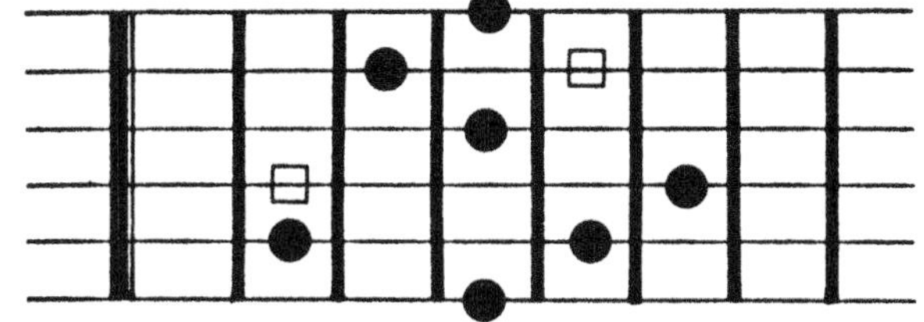

E9 arpeggio

Adding the 9th scale step (F#)

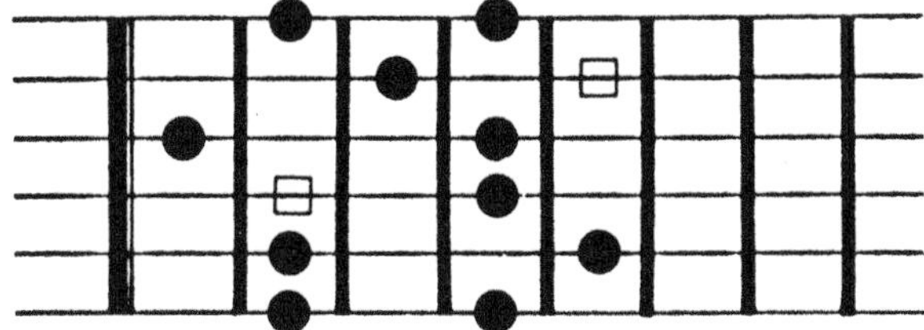

E13 arpeggio

Adding the 13th (or 6th) scale step (C#)

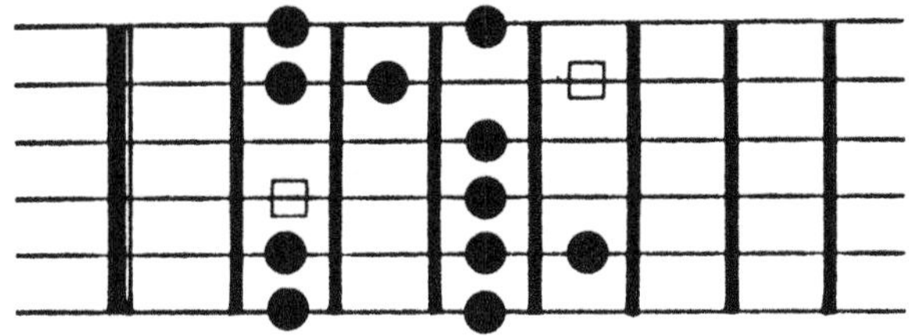

Scales & Arpeggios are essentially the same thing and end up in the same places

If we take the C major Diatonic scale C, D, E, F, G, A and B and build on it by adding thirds continually on top of C, we have C to E, E to G, G to B, B to D, D to F and F to A (all degrees of thirds--C, E, G, B, D, F and A). All in the C major scale but arranged in a different sequence:

Now take a G13 chord, this is built on the 5th degree of the C major Diatonic scale and has the notes G, B, D, F A, C, and E. Notice the same C major scale but in a different sequence.

Now lets practice this G13 arpeggio in the example below and see where it takes us.

From the root position play the third melodically ascending and descending.

Root Position

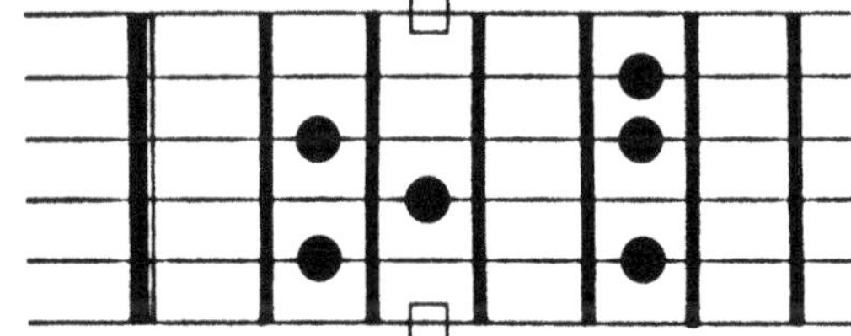

For the first inversion, we'll start on the 3rd of the scale (B), and invert the root (G) up one octave, puting it in the correct sequence within the arpeggio.

First Inversion

For the second inversion, start on the 5th of the scale (D) and invert the 3rd (B) and the root (G) up one octave.

Second Inversion

For the third inversion, start on the lowered 7th of the scale (F) and invert the root, 3rd and 5th up one octave.

Third Inversion

Notice that this third inverted arpeggio is the Diatonic C major scale starting on the F note (also called the F Lydian mode).

Having fun? Experiment with these arpeggios by adding the lowered 5ths and raised 9ths all the way to the 13th chord.

Foreign and Exotic Scales

I have included these scales for those wishing to impress their friends and loved ones, but for the serious music student you'll find much hidden within them, particularly in the extraction of their scale-tone chords. For the fingering you're on you're own.

Lydian Minor
Overtone
Leading Whole Tone
Arabian
Balinese
Chinese
Gypsy
Mohammedan
Javanese
Persian
Algerian
Aeolian
Byzantine
Hawaiian
Jewish
Mongolian
Ethiopian
Spanish
Egyptian
Japanese

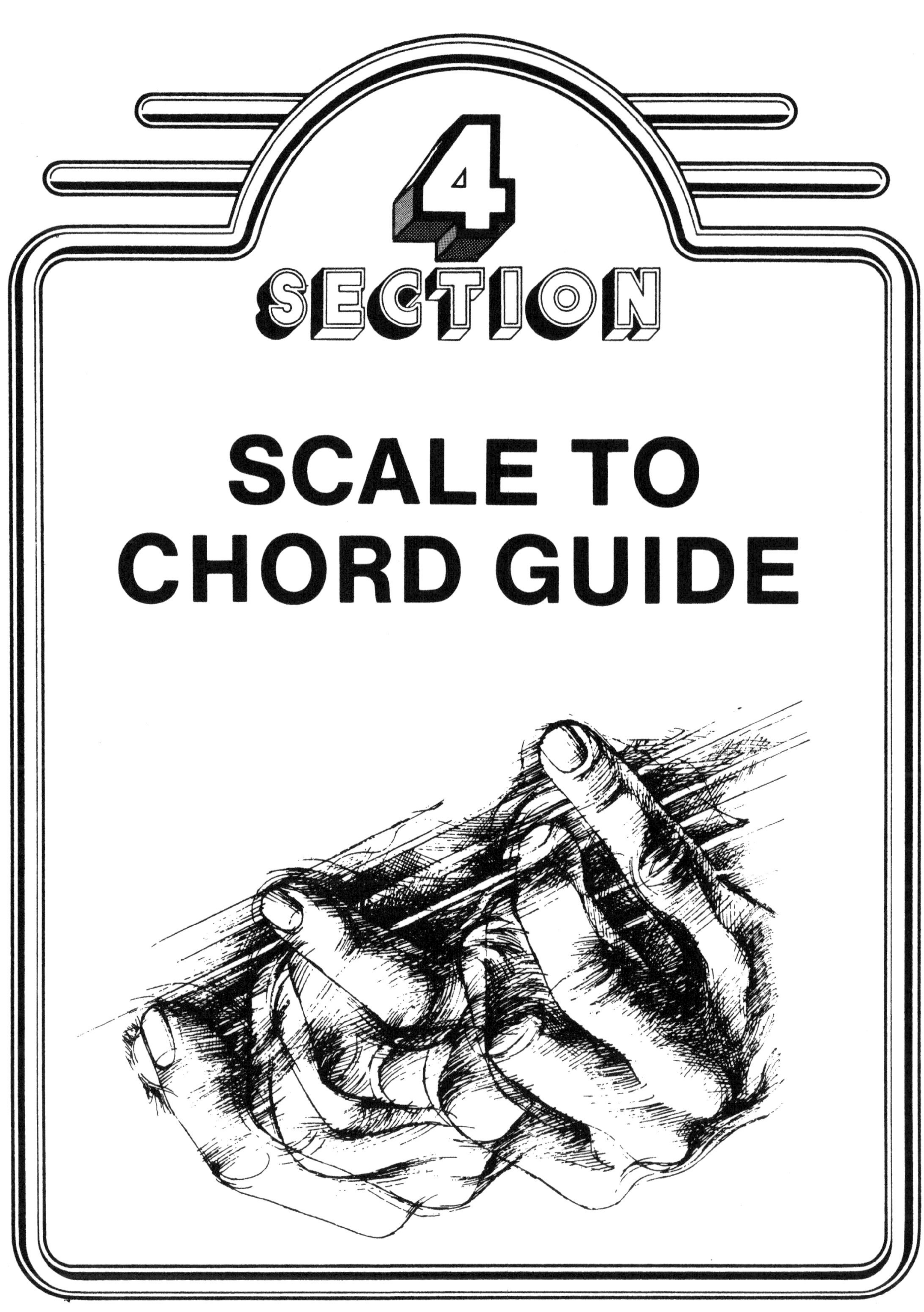
4
SECTION
SCALE TO
CHORD GUIDE

Guide To Scale Choice
Major Family

Chord Type and Chord Scale Steps	Chord Symbol key of C	Appropriate Scale Form
Major 1 3 5	C	Major Pentatonic Minor Pentatonic Major scale
Major 7th 1 3 5 7	C maj.7 C△7 CM7 C 7	Major Lydian Minor Pentatonic on the 3rd Minor Pentatonic on the 7th 6th Mode, Harmonic Minor
Major sixth 1 3 5 6	C6	Major Pentatonic
Major ninth 1 3 5 7 9	Cmaj.9 CM9 C△9	Major scale Lydian mode
Major 6-9 1 3 (5) 6 9	C6/9	Major Pentatonic Major scale
Add nine 1 3 5 9	Cadd9	Major scale Lydian mode 6th Mode, Harmonic Minor
Major 7th,b5 1 3 b5 7	Cmaj7b5 Cmaj7-5 CM7b5	Lydian Minor Pentatonic on the 7th
Major 7th,#5 1 3 #5 7	Cmaj7 #5 C△7#5 CM7 #5	Lydian Augmented Augmented 3rd Mode, Harmonic Minor
Major Thirteenth 1 3 5 7 (9) 13	Cmaj13 C△13	Major scale Lydian Mode
Suspended second 1 2 5 Suspended Fourth 1 4 5	Csus2 Cs2 Csus4 Cs4	Major Pentatonic add 4th, no third
Major Triad,sus4 1 4 5	Csus4	Major Minor Pentatonic on the 2nd
Major Seven, Sharp Eleventh 1 3 5 7 (9) #11	Cmaj 7#11 C△7#11	Lydian Mode

Guide To Scale Choice
Minor Family

Chord Type and Chord Scale Steps	Chord Symbol key of C	Appropriate Scale Form
Minor 1 b3 5	Cmin. Cm C-	Minor Pentatonic Dorian Mode Aeolian Mode
Minor 7th, Tonic (1) Function 1 b3 5 b7	Cmin7 Cm7 C-7	Dorian Aeolian Minor Pentatonic Minor Pentatonic on the 5th Blues Phrygian 4th Mode, Harmonic Minor
Minor 6th or 6-9 1 b3 5 6 1 b3 (5) 6 9	Cmin6 Cm6 Cmin6/9 Cm6 9	Dorian Melodic Minor Minor Pentatonic Blues
Minor 7th, Supertonic (II) function 1 b3 5 b7	Cmin7 Cm7 C-7	Dorian Minor Pentatonic Blues Whole Step-Half Step Diminishe
Minor 7th,III or VI function 1 b3 5 b7	Cmin7 Cm7	Aeolian Phrygian
Minor 7th, sus4 1 b3 4 b7	Cm7 sus4 Cm7 +4	Dorian Minor Pentatonic Minor Pentatonic on the 5th
Minor,#7 1 b3 5 7	Cm/maj7 Cm#7 Cm (m7) Cm△7	Ascending Melodic Minor Harmonic Minor
Minor 9 1 b3 5 b7 9	Cmin9 Cm9 C-9	Minor Pentatonic Dorian Mode Aeolian Mode
Minor Eleventh 1 b3 5 b7 (9) 11	Cmin11 Cm11 C-11	Minor Pentatonic Dorian Mode Aeolian Mode
Minor Thirteenth 1 b3 5 b7 (9) (11) 13	Cmin 13 Cm13 C-13	Minor Pentatonic Dorian Mode
Minor Seven Flat Five (Half Diminished) 1 b3 b5 b7	Cm 7b5 Cm 7-5 CØ	Locrian Mode

Guide to Scale Choice
Dominant Family

Chord Type and Chord Scale Steps	Chord Symbol key of C	Appropriate Scale Form
Dominant 7th, unaltered 1 3 5 b7	C7	Mixolydian Lydian, b7 Major Pentatonic
Dominant 7th, b5or #11 1 3 b5 b7 or 1 3 b7 #11	C7 b5 C7 #11	Lydian, b7
Dominant 7th, b5 or #5 or both 1 3 b5 #5 b7	C7 b5 #5	Whole Tone
Dominant 7th, b9 1 3 5 b7 b9	C7 b9 C7-9	Half Step-Whole Step Diminished 5th Mode, Harmonic Minor
Dominant 7th, #9 1 3 5 b7 #9	C7 #9	Half Step-Whole Step Diminished Dorian Blues Minor Pentatonic
Dominant 7th, b9 #9 1 3 5 b7 b9 #9	C7 b9 #9	Half Step-Whole Step Diminished
Dominant 7th, altered 5th or 9th (any combination) 1 3 b5 b7----1 3 5 b7 #9 1 3 #5 b7----1 3 5 b7 b9 etc.	C7 b5 C7 #5 C7 b9 C7 #9 C7 b5 #9 etc.	Super Locrian Minor Pentatonic on the b3rd Major Pentatonic on the b5th Whole Tone
Dominant 7th, sus4 1 4 5 b7	C7 sus4 C7 #4	Mixolydian Minor Pentatonic on the 2nd Minor Pentatonic on the 5th
Ninth 1 3 5 b7 9	C9 C7 add9	Mixolydian Mode
Eleventh 1 (3) 5 b7 (9) 11	C11	Mixolydian Mode
Thirteenth 1 3 5 b7 (9) (11) 13	C13	Mixolydian Mode

Guide To Scale Choice Half-Diminished Chords

Chord Type and Chord Scale Steps	Chord Symbol key of C	Appropriate Scale Form
Half-Diminished 1 b3 b5 b7	Cm7 -5	Locrian Locrian,#2 2nd Mode, Harmonic Minor Whole Step-Half Step Diminished
Minor 9th b5 1 b3 b5 b7 9	Cm9 b5 Cm9 -5	Locrian, #2

Diminished Chord

Chord Type and Chord Scale Steps	Chord Symbol key of C	Appropriate Scale Form
Diminished 7th 1 b3 b5 bb7	Cdim.7 C7dim.	Whole Step-Half Step Diminished 7th Mode, Harmonic Minor

Augmented Chord

Chord Type and Chord Scale Steps	Chord Symbol key of C	Appropriate Scale Form
Augmented 1 3 #5	Caug. C +	Whole Tone Diminished/Whole Tone

"In improvising you must be able to construct the scale in any direction from any starting point WITHOUT RELYING ON A FINGER PATTERN"

STYLISTIC GUITAR FOLIOS

ACOUSTIC BLUES GUITAR

by Kenny Sultan

This book/CD pack for intermediate-level players incorporates slide or bottleneck playing in both open and standard tunings. All songs are primarily fingerstyle with a monotone bass used for most.

00000157 Book/CD Pack $18.95
00000336 DVD $19.95

BLUES GUITAR

by Kenny Sultan

Through instructional text and actual songs, the author covers blues in five different keys and positions. Covers fingerstyle blues, specific techniques, open tuning, and bottleneck guitar. The CD includes all songs and examples, most played at slow speed and at regular tempo.

00000283 Book/CD Pack $17.95

BLUES GUITAR LEGENDS

by Kenny Sultan

This book/CD pack allows you to explore the styles of Lightnin' Hopkins, Blind Blake, Mississippi John Hurt, Blind Boy Fuller, and Big Bill Broonzy. Through Sultan's arrangements, you will learn how studying the masters can help you develop your own style.

00000181 Book/CD Pack $19.95
00000193 VHS Video $19.95

CHRISTMAS SOUTH OF THE BORDER

featuring the Red Hot Jalapeños with special guest The Cactus Brothers

Add heat to your holiday with these ten salsa-flavored arrangements of time-honored Christmas carols. With the accompanying CD, you can play your guitar along with The Cactus Brothers on: Jingle Bells • Deck the Halls • Silent Night • Joy to the World • What Child Is This? • and more. ¡Feliz Navidad!

00000319 Book/CD Pack $19.95

A CLASSICAL CHRISTMAS

by Ron Middlebrook

This book/CD pack features easy to advanced play-along arrangements of 23 top holiday tunes for classical/fingerstyle guitar. Includes: Birthday of a King • God Rest Ye, Merry Gentlemen • Good Christian Men, Rejoice • Jingle Bells • Joy to the World • O Holy Night • O Sanctissima • What Child Is This? (Greensleeves) • and more. The CD features a demo track for each song.

00000271 Book/CD Pack $15.95

ESSENTIAL BLUES GUITAR

by Dave Celentano

This handy guide to playing blues guitars emphasizes the essentials, such as: chord changes, scales, rhythms, turn arounds, phrasing, soloing and more. Includes lots of examples, plus 10 rhythm tracks for soloing and improvising.

00000237 Book/CD Pack $19.95

FINGERSTYLE GUITAR

by Ken Perlman

Teaches beginning or advanced guitarists how to master the basic musical skills of fingerpicking techniques needed to play folk, blues, fiddle tunes or ragtime on guitar.

00000081 Book Only $24.95
00000175 VHS Video $24.95

THE FLATPICKER'S GUIDE

by Dan Crary

This instruction/method book for flatpicking teaches how to play accompaniments, cross-picking, and how to play lick strums. Examples in the book are explained on the accompanying CD. The CD also allows the player to play along with the songs in the book.

00000231 Book/CD Pack $19.95

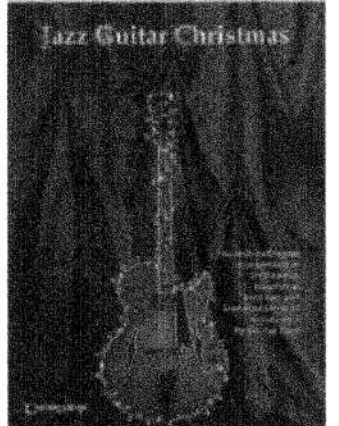

JAZZ GUITAR CHRISTMAS

by George Ports

Features fun and challenging arrangements of 13 Christmas favorites. Each song is arranged in both easy and intermediate chord melody style. Songs include: All Through the Night • Angels from the Realm of Glory • Away in a Manger • The Boar's Head Carol • The Coventry Carol • Deck the Hall • Jolly Old St. Nicholas • and more.

00000240 ......$9.95

JAZZ GUITAR SOLOS

by George Ports and Frank Sibley

Jazz horn players are some of the best improvisers ever. Now guitarists can learn their tricks! This book features 12 solos (progressing in difficulty) from jazz saxophonists and trumpeters transcribed in easy-to-read guitar tab. The CD features each solo played twice, at slow and regular tempo.

00000188 Book/CD Pack $19.95

THE NASTY BLUES

by Tom Ball

A celebration of crude and lewd songs by the best bluesmen and women in history, including Bo Carter, Bessie Smith, Irene Scruggs, Lil Johnson, Georgia White, Charlie Pickett, Lonnie Johnson, Ethel Waters, Dirty Red, and more. 30 songs in all, including: Sam, The Hot Dog Man • I Need a Little Sugar in My Bowl • Send Me a Man • Empty Bed Blues • One Hour Mama • and more.

00000049 ......$12.95

THE PATRIOTIC GUITARIST

arranged by Larry McCabe

This red, white and cool collection contains 22 all-American guitar solos for fingerpickers and flatpickers. Includes: America the Beautiful • The Battle Hymn of the Republic • The Marines' Hymn • The Star Spangled Banner • Yankee Doodle • and many more patriotic favorites. The accompanying CD includes demo tracks for all the tunes.

00000293 Book/CD Pack $19.95

PEDAL STEEL LICKS FOR GUITAR

by Forest Rodgers

Learn to play 30 popular pedal steel licks on the guitar. All examples are played three times on the accompanying CD. Also features tips for the best steel guitar sound reproduction, and steel guitar voiced chords.

00000183 Book/CD Pack $16.95
00000348 DVD $19.95

ROCK AROUND THE CLASSICS

by Dave Celentano

This book/CD pack introduces guitarists of all levels to fresh and innovative ways of playing some of the most popular classical songs. The songs are in order from easiest to most challenging, and a lesson is included on each. Includes: Leyenda • Jesu, Joy of Man's Desiring • Prelude in C# Major • Toccata and Fugue in D Minor • Canon in D Major • more.

00000205 Book/CD Pack $19.95

THE SOUND AND FEEL OF BLUES GUITAR

by John Tapella

This comprehensive blues book features information on rhythm patterns, fingerpicking patterns, double stops, licks in A, D, E, and G, and more. The accompanying CD features several compositions and all examples in the book.

00000092 Book/CD Pack $17.95

SURF GUITAR

by Dave Celentano

This totally tubular book/CD pack gives you all the tools to play convincing surf guitar, covering concepts, techniques, equipment and even surf slang! At the core of the book are six original surf songs by The Torquays. You can play along with these six tunes on the accompanying CD, and for each one, the book includes a transcription, lesson and analysis.

00000279 Book/CD Pack $22.95

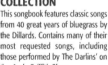

THIS IS THE TIME – THE DILLARDS SONGBOOK COLLECTION

NEW

This songbook features classic songs from 40 great years of bluegrass by the Dillards. Contains many of their most requested songs, including those performed by The Darlins' on the *Andy Griffith Show*.

00000382 ......$19.95

VIRGINIA REELS

by Joseph Weidlich

This unique book/CD pack features basic fingerstyle guitar arrangements of 35 songs originally arranged for pianoforte in George Willig, Jr.'s book *Virginia Reels*, published in Baltimore in 1839. The accompanying CD features all of the songs recorded at medium tempo and played in their entirety, and the book includes helpful performance notes.

00000241 Book/CD Pack $17.95

Book's and DVD's from Centerstream Publishing

P.O Box 17878- Anaheim Hills, CA 92817

centerstrm@aol.com